Additional Praise for *Exploring Theology*

"*Exploring Theology* invites us to consider the ways in which theology permeates all parts of our lives, regardless of whether we are fully aware of its influence. Elaine Robinson draws us into a conscientious faith by fostering deep, mature, and complex reflection. She offers a primer on the key terms and concepts of theology in a way that encourages us to articulate our own fundamental beliefs in conversation with Christian tradition. In so doing, *Exploring Theology* provides a useful beginning framework for anyone pursuing theological education on the seminary or graduate level."

Amy Levad
University of St. Thomas

"Theology can be a daunting discipline for newcomers. Elaine Robinson's primer translates the core questions and concepts of theology into a language that is accessible and engaging. *Exploring Theology* represents the ideal starting point for students wanting to know what theology is and how to do it."

Todd Green
Luther College

"Elaine Robinson has given us a clear-headed introduction to the what, why, and how of theological reflection. Here critical reflection is fully compatible with real, living faith. These pages provide a useful map for the discovery 'faith seeking understanding,' which great theologians have always practiced. This book presents an informed and encouraging starting point for the study of theology for seminary students and, I would hope, for serious study groups across the whole range of Christian churches."

Don E. Saliers
Candler School of Theology, Emory University

FOUNDATIONS FOR LEARNING

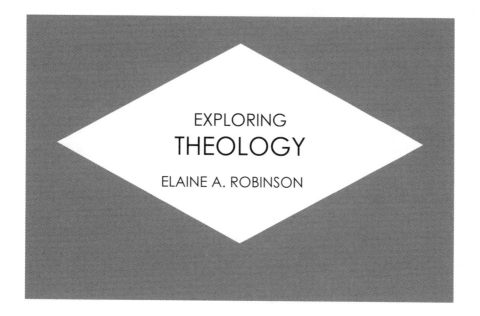

EXPLORING
THEOLOGY

ELAINE A. ROBINSON

EXPLORING THEOLOGY

Cover design: Laurie Ingram
Book design: PerfecType, Nashville, TN

Library of Congress Cataloging-in-Publication Data is available
Print ISBN: 978-1-4514-8891-3
eBook ISBN: 978-1-4514-8961-3

The paper used in this publication meets the minimum requirements of American National Standard for Information Sciences — Permanence of Paper for Printed Library Materials, ANSI Z329.48-1984.

Manufactured in the U.S.A.

Contents

Introduction

In 1990, I was an officer in the United States Air Force stationed at the Air Force Academy just outside Colorado Springs. I was serving as a professor teaching political science to the cadets, college students preparing to become Air Force officers. During that time, I was deeply involved in my local congregation in the city, attending services, Sunday school, and Wednesday-evening programming. When I arrived at church one Wednesday evening in January 1991, the fellowship hall was filled with people gathered around a television set, watching the first bombs and missiles of Operation Desert Storm. Until that moment, for some eight years, I had served in a peacetime Air Force, primarily as a manager of aircraft launch and repair operations on fighter jets. Now we were at war, and my mind was racing. Had I not been assigned to teach at the academy, I most likely would have been deployed with a squadron of fighter jets dropping bombs in the Persian Gulf.

The more I placed my Christian faith in conversation with my career as an Air Force officer, the more questions I began to have. I believe in a just-war theory—the notion that there are particular criteria that can help us to assess the moral justification for going to war—and I have never been so naive as to think that peaceful means will always prevail in a broken world. But I had never directly confronted my potential participation in the taking of human life, even if for the greater good. I remember going to teach my classes, where we had academic freedom to explore and question, and asking the cadets, "When you came to the academy, did anyone ask

1

you if you're willing to give your life for your country?" "Yes, Ma'am!" they would all reply. Then I would ask, "And when you came to the academy, did anyone ask if you're willing to take a life for your country?" That is, of course, the other side of the equation, and we should all carefully consider the implications before accepting a commission into the armed forces.

In my own life and spirit, I had come to a turning point. I knew I could not answer the second question in the affirmative. I was not comfortable taking lives on behalf of my country, even as I would be grateful for those who could do so in times of true national emergency. And as this realization grew within me and I knew it was time to resign my commission, I also began to feel a powerful calling into the ministry of the church. At the time, I could not see myself as an ordained minister, administering the sacraments and proclaiming the gospel on a weekly basis. But I could envision myself as a seminary professor, as a layperson fulfilling a vital ministry of the church. Soon I would be leaving the Air Force and heading to seminary to begin a journey that, ultimately, did lead to ordination and time as the pastor of local congregations. Only now, as I look back upon my call into ministry—or any person's call to serve Christ as a lay- or clergyperson—I am profoundly aware of the multiple ways in which theology was shaping and guiding my thoughts, decisions, and actions. Theology is the substance of our lives in God, whether we are conscious of its presence and function or largely unaware of its influence.

The word *theology* comes from the Greek words *Theos* (God) and *logos* (word, discourse). Simply put, theology is God-talk, the study of God and the things of faith. It is a reflective process in which we consider the beliefs or teachings (doctrines) of the Christian faith, how they relate one to another, how they developed, and how they are applied in each generation anew. To study theology is to undertake a journey that engages our hearts, minds, spirits, and bodies as we grow in understanding and in accepting the mystery that shrouds the fullness of God. We finite human beings do not possess the capacity to grasp the fullness of God. Psalm 8, for example, declares:

> When I look at your heavens, the work of your fingers,
>   the moon and the stars that you have established;
> what are human beings that you are mindful of them,
>   mortals that you care for them? (Ps. 8:3-4)

Remember to pause and learn the terms that are new and unfamiliar to you. As you build your theological vocabulary, the study of theology will become easier.

Similarly, Paul writes to the Corinthians that we "see in a mirror, dimly" (1 Cor. 13:12), as our human understanding is limited by our finitude. Like an ocean, God is wider and deeper and vastly more complex than is evident from the shore or even aboard a boat skimming the surface of the waters.

Theology is like a stream or various streams emanating from different geographical points all flowing toward that deep and vast ocean, teeming with an abundance of life. I invite you, as you enter into this journey, to imagine yourself carried along by a stream, now beginning to swim and dive, to consciously navigate the waters, discovering more than what lies simply on the surface as you float along. Imagine that theology is a stream into which we dip our toes and then perhaps leap, becoming immersed. In so doing, we can begin to navigate this stream that carries us ever deeper into the vast ocean that is the fullness of God, an ocean we can never map or contain fully, an ocean that will continually reveal new mysteries and wonders to us, if we are open to the journey.

Of course, as with any ocean voyage, there may be moments when the waters become turbulent and we feel ourselves threatened or unsettled and wish only to cling to the side of the boat or the shore, thinking that there we will remain grounded or safe and secure, when in fact, the ocean itself is what we are seeking. Consider the text of Matt. 14:22-33, where the disciples find themselves on a rough sea and, after a long night, are shocked to see Jesus come toward them, walking on the water. Most of the disciples cling to the side of the boat, maybe even settling deeper into the hull. Can you imagine them peeking over the side? But not Peter. He takes the risk of faith to climb out and step onto the water, yearning to draw nearer to Jesus. Of course, when he forgets that this journey is about God and the power of God at work in human lives, he slips and becomes frightened. Jesus does not let him sink but reaches out and lifts him up again to continue the journey of drawing closer to the living God in mind, body, spirit, and heart.

Peter's longing to go deeper and his willingness to step out of his comfort zone for the sake of growing his faith provide a model for our journey into theology. Many persons choose to stay within the safe confines of the theology they learned as children in Sunday school. But the human being is created with a capacity to learn, grow, and mature across a lifetime. The Gospel of Luke tells us that Jesus himself began to study as a young boy and grew in "wisdom and in years" (Luke 2:52) before beginning his ministry to the world. Moreover, Jesus was always asking questions. Those of us who take the risk of faith and, like Peter, get out of the boat and take a few bold steps to know Christ more fully will mature as disciples of Jesus Christ. Our thirst for God will become stronger and bolder. Our hunger for God will not be easily satisfied by the ordinary diet of platitudes such as "Jesus loves you" or "It is God's will." Those of us willing and eager to get out of the boat will discover an unimaginable beauty in the mystery and complexity of life in God, a hunger and thirst that will grow in our longing for a fuller relationship with God. We are reminded of the words of Saint Augustine, the bishop of Hippo, who wrote in his *Confessions* centuries ago that our hearts are restless until they rest in God.

If your heart is restless, if your mind thirsts and hungers to know the living God more deeply, then the study of theology will fill you with delight and excitement. Theological understanding will energize you and equip you for more compassionate and thoughtful ministry. In the pages that follow, we will begin this journey of consciously exploring our theology. Although we can only begin to study the vast ocean, this small volume should provide you with a map to consult as you shove off from shore and encounter the wonders of theology.

Our starting point is simple. The first thing we need to grasp is the practice often called "critical reflection." *Critical* does not here mean that we are disapproving of the beliefs we encounter; the word is not used pejoratively. Rather, critical reflection implies that we take our life in God so seriously that we are compelled to give careful examination to our faith and our teachings—to test the spirits (1 John 4:1), in a manner of speaking. Another way of understanding critical reflection is through the terminology offered by seminary professors Howard Stone and James Duke in their helpful introduction to theological reflection, *How to Think Theologically*. Stone and Duke demonstrate the difference between "embedded theology" and "deliberative theology."[1] Embedded theology is, at heart, the preconceived notions we hold about God and the life of faith, but without conscious consideration of these beliefs. We may have learned them in church, from our family, from television preachers, or even by means of social media. The sources of these deeply held assumptions can be wide and varied. But our embedded theology has not been brought to light and carefully considered.

By contrast, deliberative theology is a form of questioning, of inquiring about those beliefs we hold. For example, if we often respond to situations with the phrase "It is God's will," deliberative theology will begin to ask questions. Why would God will such a thing? Are there competing claims about what God's will might be, such as God's desire that we might have life abundantly? What about human free will? Does it play a role in situations? These represent just a few questions we might begin to ask when engaging in deliberative theology. When we examine our beliefs, rather than cast doubt upon them, we are more faithful to seek the living God. We become more humble before the mystery and immensity of the divine. We recognize that the life of faith is a journey of discovery, and just as Jesus asked his disciples, we are asked to question and consider what it means to believe in God, follow Christ, and serve others in a world that is far from perfect. We honor the living God by engaging the practice of deliberative theology and seeking to know the Triune God more fully.

 Familiarize yourself with the definition of theology, as well as the terms *embedded* and *deliberative theology.*

I invite you, then, to come along with me on this journey of seeking to know the living God more fully by entering into the practice of reflecting on our faith. While this book is designed for those who are exploring a call to seminary and full-time ministry, anyone interested in going deeper into the study of theology will benefit from this journey of the head and heart. If we return to our metaphor of diving into a stream that leads toward the ocean that is the fullness of God, then this book will provide you with navigational aids to make the journey more manageable. Throughout this book, I will introduce you to theological vocabulary. These are key words or ideas with which you should be familiar, and they are defined in the text as they are introduced. As with any discipline or area of study, the more fluent we are in the vocabulary, the easier the subject matter becomes. I encourage you to pause on the key terms and develop a working definition in your own mind. If need be, consult a theological dictionary or textbook to clarify the definition. This practice will go a long way toward your development of a deliberative theology.

In chapter 1, we will spend some time defining theology and mapping out the various branches of theological inquiry. Then chapter 2 of our journey takes us through a brief history of how the church's doctrines have developed, with key questions and thinkers introduced. You will find an occasional excerpt from the writings of a key theologian, so that you might begin to grasp how reading theology can be not just an intellectual

 Read through the table of contents, which will provide you with an overview of the contents of this book. The table of contents is always a bit of a map that will help to guide your reading and study.

exercise, but also a spiritual practice. This overview of some of the streams of theology present in our churches and world today should help you locate your own starting point for doing theology. We will refer to these streams as "theological movements."

In chapter 3, we will begin to explore the structure of theological reflection or the sources and method for articulating our faith. As Jesus says in the gospel of Luke 14:28, "For which of you, intending to build a tower, does not first sit down and estimate the cost?" In doing theology, we want to understand the materials needed and sketch a basic pattern for our theological journey before we begin to construct it. Chapter 3 also includes a discussion of the importance of language to theology and what I refer to as "expansive" language when speaking of God.

Then in chapter 4, we turn to a basic overview of the "content" of the Christian faith, the doctrines or doctrinal loci that provide a systematic arrangement of our beliefs. Not only will we sketch the basic teachings of the Christian faith, but our goal is to also see the relevance of these teachings for today. This work will then enable you to write your own first and provisional credo, or statement of what you believe. In other words, this journey is not intended to tell you what or how to believe, but to give you the tools to articulate your own most deeply held beliefs about God and the life of faith. This goal is the heart of theology: to enable each person to express for himself or herself a thoughtful, careful understanding of the

Christian faith from where he or she stands in the world. At the end of this journey, in the conclusion, I will close with suggestions for continuing the study of theology beyond these first steps.

The ocean lies in the distance. The roar of the waves is barely discernible to our ears. The faint smell of saltwater reaches our nostrils, and the sticky, humid air lies gently upon our skin. Our eyes scan the horizon for the first signs of the vast, powerful sea with all its wonder and mystery. But for now, we are floating gently on a raft, ready to pick up the oars and begin charting a path toward that distant ocean. Our journey into theology has now begun.

 ## Questions for Personal Exploration

1. What does "theology" mean? How have you already been doing theology, even before picking up this book?
2. What is the difference between embedded and deliberative theology? Can you think of a time when you engaged in deliberative theology? What led you into that reflective mode, and where did it take you?
3. What excites you about beginning the study of theology? What fears might you bring to this journey?

 ## Resources for Deeper Exploration

Harvey, Van A. *A Handbook of Theological Terms: Their Meaning and Background Exposed in Over 300 Articles.* New York: Touchstone, 1997. Or choose another dictionary of theological terms.

Stone, Howard W., and James O. Duke. *How to Think Theologically.* 3rd ed. Minneapolis: Fortress Press, 2013.

 ## Notes

1. Howard W. Stone and James O. Duke, *How to Think Theologically*, 3rd ed. (Minneapolis: Fortress Press, 2013).

Chapter 1

What Is Theology?

Theology (Greek: *Theos* + *logos*) is the study of God, our language or discourse about and reflection upon God and the Christian faith as a whole. It is an intellectual examination and accounting of what Christians believe, but with an eye toward how we practice that faith in the world. Our theology becomes expressed in our lives through our embodied practices. When we speak of "God," the divine mystery that is deeper and wider than our human understanding and imagination, we are encouraged to remember that all of our thinking and speaking about the life of faith emanates from this one reality we call God. To use a scriptural phrase, God is the Alpha and Omega, the beginning and end of all that exists (Rev. 21:6). Thus, the study of God can be thought of as the study of the whole of the life of faith. Everything we teach as Christians is, at heart, theology or God-talk.

But why do we teach about God and enter into theological reflection? Perhaps the best answer is this: We consider the life of faith and the fullness of this divine reality in order to make sense of our lives in this world and to share this knowledge or wisdom with others. We want to know who God is, who we are, how to live a good and full life, and what we are called to be and to do. All of our theological reflection, then, is a process of meaning making. To understand who God is and how we relate to the divine is to make our lives meaningful, to make sense out of this human journey. When we know how to live, then we have the possibility of living life fully and joyfully. We might say that our theology gives us a way of viewing the world in order to live abundantly. Christians believe that this is the way that leads to life.

In the introduction, we distinguished between embedded and deliberative theology. The study of theology enables us to become conscious of our most deeply held beliefs and to ask ourselves if they are actually making sense of the world, especially in light of what we know to be true about God. Take the example of someone who uses the phrase "It is God's will" as a response to everything that happens. The person finds a ten-dollar bill, and it is deemed to be God's will. He runs into an old friend at the grocery store: God's will. He gets a new job: God's will. He helps someone change a flat tire: God's will. He learns of a soldier's death: God's will. A neighbor's child dies tragically: God's will. The next town is destroyed by a flood: God's will. It is easy to ascribe everything that happens in our lives to God and God's will, but such a response reflects embedded, unexamined theology. Let's explore how this response to the various situations of our lives might unravel as we begin to ask questions about and reflect upon God, the human being, and the world in which we live.

If we consider for a moment the most extreme sort of tragedy, what are the questions we might want to ask? Imagine a tornado sweeps through a town and levels neighborhood after neighborhood, resulting in the loss of life and the destruction of countless homes and businesses. What does it say about God to suggest that this sort of devastation is God's will? It would suggest, at the very least, that God seeks to destroy and bring death. Now we need to ask: Why would God send Jesus into the world to redeem it, only to wreak great pain and suffering upon everyone indiscriminately? Doesn't this contradict the scriptural claims that God is love, that God intends abundant life, that God is good, and that God is just? Given that we know something of God's nature, how does it make sense to suggest that a tornado of such tremendous destructive force is God's will?

So if it is not simply God's will, then what about punishment? We have all heard Christian interpreters who claim that such destructive events are God's punishment for one supposed societal sin or another. But again, when we begin to question this claim in the light of what we know to be true about God, the pronouncement begins to unravel. Does a punishing God indiscriminately take the lives of the guilty and innocent alike? Doesn't God view all sin as disobedience? Why would God single out one form of sin over any other? Why does God seem to punish whatever human condition the television evangelist himself most dislikes? Doesn't the Bible say, "Judge not that ye be not judged"? (Matt. 7:1) Doesn't it seem strange that God, out of deep love, would send Jesus Christ to redeem us but then continue to use death and destruction as a means of punishment? What about Jesus' own words that he came to bring life and life abundantly?

Thus, when we ask careful and thoughtful questions in relationship to what we know from the Scriptures, our Christian heritage, our experience, and by means of reasoned analysis, when we move toward deliberative theology, we begin to recognize that perhaps what is going on isn't God's will or God's punishment, but rather something else quite tragic. Does your faith include a belief in a fallen world that God in Christ is working to redeem? Does your faith include a belief in natural evil apart from moral evil? Perhaps the tornado isn't God's will or God's punishment for one supposed sin after all, but points toward the reality of a world that is not yet the new creation and continues to be riddled with suffering and evil.

In these few paragraphs, we have only begun to think theologically about the phrase "It is God's will" and how deliberative theology, our conscious examination of our beliefs, begins to unravel the phrase's ability to make sense of our world. In these paragraphs, you have already started to explore questions of theodicy (the problem of evil), natural evil, the nature of God, Christology, and eschatology (the last things). In chapter 4, we will return to this question of why terrible things happen in our world and develop an even deeper deliberative theology. But at this point, several things should be clear. First, our *unexamined* beliefs and expressions of faith can do as much harm as good. Second, we are all theologians in a very real sense. We are all speaking of and trying to making sense of God and God's presence and will for humanity and the whole of creation. We are trying to make sense of our human lives. Yet the quality of that theological reflection may differ greatly. Third, the more carefully we begin to explore questions of faith, the more exciting, meaningful, and faithful our Christian journey becomes. Rather than somehow undermining our faith, this process of asking questions leads us into a deeper and richer relationship with God, as well as a more fulfilling life in the world. It makes us better able to be in ministry to others. We might say, to use a Pauline reference, we take on the "mind of Christ" (1 Cor. 2:16).

Having whetted your appetite to think theologically, I want to help you grasp how this practice of theology entered into common usage among

Christians, as well as to distinguish the different ways the word *theology* is used, since the ambiguity can sometimes lead to confusion among new students of theology.

The Limits of Our Knowledge of God

I teach in a seminary, preparing students for full-time ministries of the church. Sometimes, as seminarians begin this process of preparation, they find the term *theology* quite confusing, and rightly so. While the study of theology is an engaging and exciting process, it can also be difficult. This kind of critical, reflective thinking may be new to many entering into the study of theology, especially those who have not previously studied the humanities and philosophy. Because God is spirit and infinite, we are unable to directly observe and describe the divine reality. Historically, this has been encapsulated by the Latin phrase used by John Calvin, *finitum non*

 Review and understand the significance of the phrase *finitum non est capax infiniti.*

est capax infiniti, translated as "The finite cannot contain the infinite." We are limited in our physical and intellectual capacities, as well as by time and space, but God is limitless. We are, each of us, a little container of life that can only hold a sliver of the fullness of God within. As a result, the language we use to speak of God is always indirect, or by way of metaphor and analogy (a subject to which we will return in chapter 3). For this reason, some students find theology to be rather abstract. And for those who seek to be taught "the" answer to difficult theological questions, theology becomes disappointing, since the deeper we dig, the fewer absolute answers we are able to formulate, and the more questions we are compelled to ask.

Of course, this sense of uncertainty and mystery should not surprise us, given that we human beings are finite or limited creatures and, as 1 Cor. 13:12 reminds us, we see in a mirror dimly and know only in part. In this life, our understanding is necessarily limited by our creatureliness, and we are called to remain humble and open before the vastness that is God and the life of faith. If you find yourself struggling with the abstract nature of theology, wanting more concrete answers and certainty, it may be helpful to remind yourself of this biblical claim that now we see only in part. We are not created with the capacity to understand the fullness of God, though we are able to grasp the contours of what God has revealed to humanity through the Scriptures and Jesus of Nazareth. We are able to touch only the hem of God's garment, much like Isaiah's vision of encountering the living God in the temple (Isa. 6:1).

Thus, we human creatures, gifted with consciousness and yearning to know God, can never become like God, having complete knowledge and understanding. One of the most poignant stories in the Bible is found in Genesis 2:4—3:24, which recounts the second creation story and what we traditionally refer to as "the fall," in which the man and woman together commit the original sin or the first act of turning away from God. It is an etiological tale, a tale that answers the question: How did we get into the human situation in which we find ourselves? In early generations and sometimes, unfortunately, in the present day, the "blame" has often been placed upon the woman, who actually takes from the tree of the knowledge of good and evil in the middle of the garden in what we might identify as a sin of commission. But the text clearly states that she gave some to her husband "who was with her," as if to indicate that he was watching passively, thereby committing a sin of omission. They are both culpable. But perhaps the most important point of this story has nothing to do with who is responsible for the fall. Rather, it has to do with the human desire to become "like God, knowing good and evil" (3:5). For after they eat, the man and woman do, indeed, recognize there is good and evil, but the fact that they immediately cover their nakedness, as if suddenly discovering the human body is no longer good, tells us they are unable to discern with certainty which is which— which is good and which is evil. Indeed, down through the ages, Christians have debated and continue to debate whether one thing or another is good or evil in God's sight. From the beginning, then, human beings have sought certainty and complete knowledge of God, but the Bible indicates we are not in this life capable of the fullness of God.

And so we enter into the practice of theological reflection, seeking to draw as near as possible to the reality of God and the right way to live as followers of Jesus Christ, but in an attitude of humility that recognizes we can never arrive at perfect and complete knowledge. We might just get some things wrong or not see the whole picture, much like the first people in the garden. No matter how many years we might study theology, the knowledge of God remains somewhat elusive, and our eyes are continually opened to see anew the heights and depths of God.

The Broader and Narrower Meanings of "Theology"

More pragmatically, theology can be confusing also simply because the term is used in a variety of ways. In contemporary usage, theology can refer, in a broader and more general sense, to all of the studies we undertake in preparation for various ministries. In its particular usage, theology refers to a specific area of study more precisely known as "systematic theology." In this section, we will explore the many ways in which the word *theology* may be used in the course of seminary studies, as well as provide a brief historical overview of the development of this term and of the academic discipline and ministry skill known as theology. Although this book focuses on introducing you to the academic discipline of theology commonly referred to as systematic theology, mapping the larger terrain of theological studies will help you navigate the meanings and complexity of this beautiful but confounding word, *theology*. Our brief background concerning the word's meaning can begin to unravel some of the ambiguity of this subject and practice.

As is true of many words, the meaning of *theology* has evolved and expanded over the centuries. The word *awful* is a good example. Up through the eighteenth century and even into the nineteenth, *awful* was used to express the condition of being filled with awe. Today, of course, this word tends to express something undesirable or decidedly bad, though we do still speak of having an "awfully good time," which reflects the earlier usage. To take another example from more contemporary parlance, in some circles, the word *bad* has come to mean exactly the opposite: something deemed really bad is actually quite good. Thus, understanding the meaning of any word in a particular time or culture is of great importance. So often we use words, especially in sharing our faith, that lack precision or that we do not fully understand. Ask people at your Sunday school class or a Bible study you attend to define grace or ask them what worship is, and you will get a sense of the uncertainty. But our faith depends in many ways on grasping the deeper meaning of our language of faith. Since God cannot be apprehended directly with our physical senses, the words we use about God are of primary importance.

When and how, then, did the word *theology* enter into our language as the common way of referring to the study of the teachings of the Christian faith? Although the word *theology* is Greek in origin and also found in the Latin writings of the early Christian theologians, it is not found in the New Testament, but arose out of the need to make sense of the biblical witnesses and the teachings of the early church. You may react to this knowledge by asking, "If this word is not in the Bible, then why would we use or care about it?" That is a good question, and one that has been asked for generations in various forms.

As you might suspect, the answer is a bit complicated. First, we develop words to help us better articulate the Christian faith. *Trinity* is a good example. The biblical witnesses never use this word to speak of God, yet we Christians understand that the one true God is known to us in three persons: Father, Son, and Holy Spirit (sometimes today we say Creator, Redeemer, and Sustainer to name the three persons). This Trinity is how God has revealed God's self to us, in and through the scriptural witnesses. Yet, because the Scriptures do not provide a word or language to describe this reality, early Christians began to name God as a Trinity and, more importantly, to express how God can be known in three persons and yet remain one, and only one, God. So the first reason we develop words that are not present in the Scriptures is to help us better articulate what God has revealed about our faith through them. In fact, in the early church, theology was primarily a practice of developing a deeper understanding of the Christian life through the interpretation of the biblical writings alone.

There is a second reason that words such as *theology* emerge into common usage, even though they are not used by the biblical writers. Theology is sometimes referred to as "second-order discourse," in contrast to first-order discourse, which encompasses the primary expressions of our faith, such as worship, prayer, outreach, and even the reading of Scripture. We human beings act and express our faith in a variety of ways, after which we reflect intellectually upon our Christian practices. We want to discern if we are practicing the faith in accordance with the scriptural witnesses, if our expressions are consistent in the message or the witness they offer to others, and we wish to respond to challenges that arise. Thus, the practice of theological reflection comes after or in response to our first-order faith practices—which thus renders the reflective engagement "second-order discourse." Where did this model of reflecting upon our practices arise? It is exactly the kind of reflection we see Jesus of Nazareth practicing throughout the gospels. For example, when Jesus heals the bent-over woman, the authorities challenge his decision to heal on the Sabbath (Luke 13:10-17). His practice is deemed inappropriate, according to the religious sensibilities

 Be sure you understand the difference between first-order and second-order discourse.

of first-century Judaism. But Jesus answers their condemnation with a question: "Does not each of you on the sabbath untie his ox or his donkey from the manger, and lead it away to give it water? And ought not this woman, a daughter of Abraham whom Satan bound for eighteen long years, be set free from this bondage on the sabbath day?" (Luke 13:15-16).

Thus, when we question why the word *theology* does not appear in the Bible, we can conclude that the practice of theology was modeled for us by Jesus, Paul, and others. Theological reflection serves as a way to deepen our faith and to enable us to assess our faithfulness to the scriptural witnesses. Of course, being faithful to the scriptural witnesses is more complicated than we often admit or recognize, which is a point to which we will return in the third chapter, as we discuss the sources for doing theology. Hopefully, at this point, you feel confident that a word need not be present in the Bible to be a valid Christian concept. Such is the case with the word *theology*. But now we encounter the ambiguity of the word and its varied meanings over the centuries and even in contemporary usage. As we noted, today there are two primary ways we use the word *theology*. First, it represents the larger discipline of study, encompassing all that relates to God and the Christian faith. For example, we speak of schools of theology and all the studies contained within. This overarching meaning is the general usage of the term. The second use of *theology* is to represent the specific discipline of systematic theology, a narrower area of study that examines the doctrines (i.e., teachings) of the Christian faith in their coherence, consistency, and appropriateness. A third meaning of theology is yet more precisely the doctrine of God proper, or the study of God's nature and being, and is contained within the discipline of systematic theology.

In the following section, our focus will be the two primary meanings: the larger discipline of study and the field of systematic theology. Once we map the theological landscape, you will be able navigate it with some confidence. So at this bend in the river, we turn to a brief exploration of how theology entered into our language and became a central practice of the Christian faith.[1]

The Development of the Word *Theology*

As we noted in the previous section, *theology* is not a biblical word, though it is clearly a practice that is present within the Scriptures. A good example is found in chapter 3 of the Gospel of John, where Jesus encourages Nicodemus to reflect on the meaning of faith. Paul's letters are considered to represent the first theological reflection upon the teachings of Jesus of Nazareth (remember that—even though they refer to an earlier time—the gospels were written down later than Paul's letters). In a very real sense, Paul is the first theologian, deliberately reflecting upon the teachings of Jesus and the practices of early Christians. Even so, he did not use the word *theology* itself.

In fact, in the early church up until the twelfth century, this word *theology* was seldom used by Christian writers, at least in part due to its meaning within the pagan Greek world. In that context, the term referred first to mythologies and later, in the writings of the Stoics and beyond, to a systematic reflection on the divine (i.e., the gods) with an emphasis upon analyzing the divine presence in the world, rather than considering the nature of the gods. During the patristic period, which will be discussed in more detail later in the book, the early Christian theologians were reluctant to use the Greek term, given its associations with pagan and philosophical thought. Origen (185–253 CE) is widely held to have written the first systematic theology of sorts, *On First Principles*, which examines the truth of the scriptures and how those truths connect and relate to one another, but he does not consider himself a theologian undertaking the practice of theology. It is important to recognize that the earliest Christian writers were doing theology, even though the word was not yet in common usage for this practice of reflecting upon and providing a reasoned, coherent account of the one true God. Edward Farley, a twentieth-century theologian, explains early Christian theological engagement this way: "A salvifically oriented knowledge of divine being was part of the Christian community and tradition long before it was named theology."[2] In other words, the early Christians were reflecting upon the scriptures and articulating a preliminary knowledge of God in Christ for the sake of salvation.

Because theology was centrally concerned with the biblical witnesses from the beginning of the Christian faith, these early church writers developed ways of drawing out and presenting the meaning of the scriptures. But as is true of human beings in every generation, there was not unanimity in how the scriptures should be interpreted. There were two competing schools in the patristic era—the Alexandrian school and the Antiochene school—and variations within each school.

The Alexandrian school grew out of the interpretive methods of Philo of Alexandria (20 BCE–40 CE), who utilized an allegorical method for interpreting the Hebrew Scriptures. In utilizing this method, Philo sought to discern a hidden, deeper, spiritual meaning thought to be present in every scriptural text. With the rise of Christian interpreters located in Greek Alexandria, Philo's method was appropriated by writers such as Origen, who sought to uncover the literal, moral, and spiritual or allegorical sense of each scriptural passage as a basis for reflecting upon God and the Christian life. In the Western or Latin church, the allegorical method was practiced by Augustine of Hippo, who condensed the levels of meaning into a twofold pattern of the literal/bodily/historical sense and an allegorical/spiritual/theological one. Simply put, these writers understood that there is more to the scriptural texts than meets the eye, given the spiritual nature of God and the life of faith.

Perhaps it comes as no surprise to discover that this practice of seeking the deeper or underlying meaning of biblical texts was disputed and criticized. It led to charges of *eisogesis*, a practice of reading into the text rather than drawing out the meaning therein (i.e., *exegesis*). The Antiochene school countered the method of discerning the spiritual meaning of texts by emphasizing the historical and grammatical interpretation of scripture, in order to bring out the "plain" meaning. These interpreters sought to understand the author's meaning (we might call this the original intent) and to read the language directly rather than allegorically. In other words, the Christian writers in the Antiochene school of interpretation, such as John Chrysostom (347–407 CE), held to the belief that each text has one literal meaning that is true for all persons in all ages.

Alister McGrath helps us to see the distinction between and implications of these schools by suggesting that the Antiochene school "tended to interpret relatively few Old Testament passages as referring directly to Christ, whereas the Alexandrian School regarded Christ as the hidden content of many Old Testament passages."[3] Moreover, we can see that this debate about how to interpret the scriptures continues into our own time, with some persons adhering to a strict, unwavering meaning of each text and others allowing for a wider interpretation of the Bible.

In other words, today we continue the practice of interpretation, known as hermeneutics, and we continue to debate exactly how the Scriptures should be read and interpreted, especially for the sake of our theological reflection on God and the Christian faith. At this point, you might wish to pause and consider the ways you tend to read the Bible. Do you seek to discover the one literal meaning of any passage? Do you focus on the historical realities of the text? Or do you tend to read with an eye on the spiritual meaning, especially for your own life? Perhaps your reading of the Scriptures entails some combination of the levels of interpretation.

At this point, what is important for us to remember is that from the earliest days of the church, theology drew heavily upon the biblical witnesses, but the techniques or methods for reading those texts varied among theologians, all of whom were seeking to be faithful to God. Moreover, the question of how to read the Scriptures is present in every era of theological activity down to the present day without ever arriving at a consensus on how the Scriptures ought to be read and interpreted. Of course, a careful reader will recognize that this ongoing openness reflects the mystery of the living God whom we must seek with all our heart, mind, soul, and strength but can never fully grasp and articulate. Sometimes our interpretation will be deeply meaningful and genuinely reflective of the reality of God; other times we will fall sadly short in our interpretation as a result of our human finitude. Yet we are compelled to continue this journey of seeking to know the living God and how best to live out the scriptural claims to who God is and what we are called to be and to do. In the next chapter, we will delve more deeply into the importance of Scripture as a primary source for doing theology, but for now, let's return to our consideration of how theology came into common usage and practice.

From the sixth through the twelfth centuries, during the Middle Ages or medieval era, religious orders such as the Franciscans and Dominicans were formed, and within each order, we find particular theological emphases articulated. Noted theologians were associated with these religious orders. For instance, Thomas Aquinas was a Dominican monk, and William of Ockham belonged to the Franciscans. The practice of theology continued along the trajectory begun in the patristic era and focused on developing a comprehensive account of the meaning and the content of the biblical witnesses (i.e., knowledge received by revelation) while also engaging philosophical tools or principles (i.e., knowledge discovered through the use of reason). The use of reason to articulate Christian doctrine rose to the level of a science, sacred science, during this era. Although these Christians were doing theology, they had yet to name it as such.

One important point to keep in mind is that, in many ways, their pursuit of theology was intertwined with and inseparable from their spirituality. Theology was then and continues to be an embodied practice of the whole person, rather than simply a mental exercise. Theology should shape our spirituality and vice versa. Even so, the most noted theologians of this period, writing in the twelfth century, would be charged with lapsing into mental gymnastics dealing with minutiae considered less central to the church and salvation. For example, these theologians have been accused of debating the question "How many angels can dance on the head of a pin?" In actuality, most scholars believe this question was not really a subject of debate, but was suggested by others to illuminate and discredit the medieval tendency to consider insignificant matters ad infinitum.

Toward the end of this period of theological activity, universities began to arise, and theology entered the university setting as a particular discipline of study, based in the Scriptures and philosophical reasoning, and generally referred to as *sacra doctrina* or sacred teaching. We refer to this period of theological development in the twelfth century as scholasticism, and Thomas Aquinas is the exemplar of scholastic theology. Scholastic theology was philosophical, speculative, rational, dialectical, and questioning. It sought to systematize the knowledge of God. It became, as Congar suggests, "God's *science*, that is to say, the order according to which God, in His wisdom, links all things together."[4] The theologian's task, then, was to articulate this sacred science of God as a human endeavor aimed at providing a compendium of divine knowledge. In this era, quite unlike today, the sciences were considered to be the handmaiden of theology, because any knowledge of the world and its principles was thought necessarily to provide insights into the nature of God and God's mission or work in the world. All things point to God and originate in God. For this reason, within the early universities of Europe, theology became the queen of the sciences, possessing the heights and depths of knowledge. Strange as it may seem today, the university once understood theology as the subject that unified and undergirded all other academic disciplines.

It was in the twelfth century that the word *theology* began to emerge in the senses with which we today are familiar. Theology was now used to refer to the study of God and to the discipline that engages in this scientific pursuit. The first actual use of the word is generally attributed to Peter Abelard (1079–1142), a French scholastic philosopher and theologian whose works were written in Latin, the scholarly language of the medieval world. The *Oxford English Dictionary* provides us with the etymology of *theology* within the English language: "Abelard applied the term to a philosophical treatment of the doctrines of the Christian religion, which, though at first strongly condemned, became current, and, in this sense, 'theologia' came to designate a department of academic study, the text-books of which were the Bible and the Sentences (from the Fathers) of Peter Lombard. Hence the earliest English use."[5] We have now arrived at the point, historically, where the word *theology* enters into usage in the English language. Yet even at the outset, it conveyed multiple meanings. Not only did it mean the study of the doctrine of God proper, but it also came to represent the field or discipline of theology located within the university setting and existing to provide a reasoned account of the teachings of the Christian faith.

In the wake of the Enlightenment, the onset of modernity, and the rise of the modern university, theology ceased to be the queen of the sciences. Indeed, with the advent of modern scientific methods and the decline of traditional authorities including the church, theology could no longer claim any place among the sciences. As the university sought to free itself from the shackles of authorities, including or especially religious authorities, to pursue scientific truth via reason and replicable methods, theology was viewed with suspicion, placing the study of theology on a trajectory in which the discipline has grown to be less commonly represented in contemporary universities and sometimes subject to criticism when faith is viewed as standing in opposition to science. Yet at the same time, scholars also came to understand that modern scientific and historical methods could be applied to the study of the Bible, which aided the task of theological study.

During the nineteenth century, the discipline of theology began to fragment or divide into subdisciplines and specialties. Friedrich Schleiermacher (1768–1834) offered a proposal in *A Brief Outline of the Study of Theology* (1811), which argued for the division of theology into three separate areas: philosophical, historical, and practical theology. Schleiermacher's threefold curriculum was never widely implemented, but following his initial proposal, the study of theology has come to include a variety of disciplines, including Bible, church history, theology and ethics, and the practices of ministry. Thus, since the nineteenth century, theology has come to mean a variety of disciplines generally related to the preparation for vocational ministry. This is the broader meaning of theology. Within the academic study of theology in this broader sense, there is a particular subdiscipline or specialty known as theology, most commonly named "systematic" theology, or less frequently today, "dogmatic" theology, or sometimes "constructive" theology. This is the narrower meaning of theology in today's usage. Let's explore these two contemporary meanings of theology a bit further.

The Broader Meaning of Theology

As noted in the previous section, theology in the broader sense refers to the various studies considered necessary for ministerial preparation and formation. If you visit the website for any school of theology, such as Yale Divinity School (www.divinity.yale.edu), Luther Seminary (www.luthersem.edu), or Duke Divinity School (www.divinity.duke.edu), and click on the link to the page about its master of divinity degree (the basic degree for ordination in many denominations), you will begin to notice that the word *theology* appears in several contexts. There is an "architecture" or "landscape" suggesting that theology is the overarching way of referring to ministerial studies. A school of theology (or sometimes it will be named a school of "divinity," which is synonymous with theology, though the term *divinity* was used more commonly in the past) exists to provide for the systematic and comprehensive study of the teachings and practices of the Christian faith. A school of theology is also seminary when it participates in the education of persons for ordained ministry, though not everyone who attends a theological school is pursuing a ministry in the church. People engage in the academic study of theology for various reasons. The first thing to notice,

See if you can detect a pattern or basic architecture for theological studies among these various schools, despite their differences.

then, is that theology infuses or provides coherence to the curriculum or degree programs of the seminary or theological school.

This architecture indicates an important point: All of ministry requires a certain fluency in the language of theology and the ability to reflect upon the content or teachings of the Christian faith. Whether looking back historically at the Christian tradition, considering moral and ethical questions, developing a youth ministry, offering pastoral care, or drawing out the meaning of biblical passages, theological reflection will be central to how we understand, articulate, and practice the Christian faith. Theological studies enable us to enter into the practice of deliberative theology, which is a critical skill for effective pastoral leadership. Take another look at the website for a school of theology, and try to discern how the faculty is organized into departments, areas of study, or disciplines. In some cases, the faculty may be divided into several divisions. For example, at the time of this writing, the website for Princeton Theological Seminary (www.ptsem .edu) has a drop-down tab under "Academics" that lists faculty according to the following departments: History and Ecumenics, Biblical Studies, Practical Theology, and the Theology Department (which includes ethics). You might also note that the school has an interdisciplinary department called Religion and Society, which draws upon the resources of the first

 Explore the websites of several seminaries, focusing on their curriculum and faculty divisions.

four divisions. Another example would be the Candler School of Theology at Emory University (www.candler.emory.edu). Under Candler's website's tab for faculty "listing by area," we find four divisions again, though named a bit differently: Biblical Studies, History and Interpretation of Christianity (which includes systematic theology), Christianity and Culture (which includes ethics), and Church and Ministry (i.e., practices of ministry). You might ponder, for a moment, the logic that would lead Candler to separate theology from ethics, rather than co-locating these subdisciplines.

Since Schleiermacher's first formulation of divisions in the nineteenth century, the study of theology has generally been structured in a basic five-fold pattern that includes departments or areas of Bible, history, theology and ethics, and the practices of ministry. In each of these disciplines, we engage in theological reflection. As a result, within biblical studies, we find biblical theology. Within history, we find historical theology. Within the practices of ministry, we will encounter pastoral theology, the theology of worship, and so forth. Systematic theology and theological ethics are generally understood as distinct but related academic disciplines. The former focuses on the systematic interpretation and articulation of the teachings of the faith. The latter addresses the moral life of Christians in terms of actions, behaviors, virtues, and attitudes—in other words, how to respond to ethical realities in our lives and world or live out our Christian doctrines. In sum, we might say that theology is the unifying discipline of ministerial formation.

The Narrower Meaning of Theology

Among all these forms of theology, the area most commonly referred to as systematic theology is the more particular or narrow way in which we use the term *theology*. Students enrolled in a degree program at any of these seminaries will use the language of *theology* for the classes they take in systematic theology, as in "I'm taking a theology elective this semester in Barth and Tillich" or "I'm studying Womanist theology this semester." As we will

 Review the broader and narrower senses of *theology* as used today.

encounter in subsequent chapters of this book, systematic theology provides a framework for thinking about the different facets of our Christian faith, including God, Jesus Christ, the Holy Spirit, the church, the human being, and eschatology, among other doctrines. Systematic theology will also consider questions of the sources, methods, and context for doing theology, which we refer to as prolegomena (the things said before or first). These are the tools and considerations that theologians have engaged since the earliest days of the church, even as they have been debated and reformulated through the ages.

With this basic understanding of how the word *theology* came into usage, as well as the different meanings of the word in today's usage, we are ready to go deeper into theology. In the next chapter, we survey the eras of theological activity to gain some comprehension of how theological understanding and the church's doctrines have emerged over time.

 ## Questions for Personal Exploration

1. Review the first section, which explores the statement "It is God's will." Have you ever used this phrase? In what context? Looking back with new understanding, how might you question and rethink your use of the phrase?
2. How do you react to the knowledge that not all theological words are found in the Bible? Do you think there are good reasons for us to use terms such as *Trinity* and *theology*?
3. In what sense was theology once the "queen of the sciences"? Why is this no longer the case in modern universities? Do you think this change diminishes the importance of theology to the Christian life?

 ## Resources for Deeper Exploration

Congar, Yves. *A History of Theology.* Translated and edited by Hunter Guthrie. Garden City, NY: Doubleday & Company, 1968.

Farley, Edward. *Theologia: The Fragmentation and Unity of Theological Education.* Eugene, OR: Wipf and Stock, 2001.

Oxford English Dictionary. Oxford University Press, s.v. "Theology."

 ## Notes

1. Throughout the following section, I rely upon the work of Yves Congar, *A History of Theology*, trans. and ed. Hunter Guthrie (Garden City, NY: Doubleday & Company, 1968).

2. Edward Farley, *Theologia: The Fragmentation and Unity of Theological Education* (Eugene, OR: Wipf & Stock, 2001), 33.

3. Alister E. McGrath, *Christian Theology: An Introduction*, 4th ed. (Malden, MA: Blackwell, 2007), 130.

4. Congar, *A History of Theology*, 95.

5. *Oxford English Dictionary* (OED Online, Oxford University Press), s.v. "theology," accessed June 20, 2014, http://www.oed.com/view/Entry/200388?redirectedFrom=theology.

Chapter 2

How Did Theology Develop?

Sometimes students taking their first course in systematic theology will stumble upon an idea that they think to be brilliant and original. Of course, the fact that someone has never before encountered a particular idea does not mean that it has never been considered in the course of human history. A tremendous wealth of theological reflection has been conducted through the centuries and often is at the base of our embedded theology, even though we lack familiarity with those in the past who have shaped and sharpened the beliefs we now hold and need to examine carefully and deliberatively. To engage in the practice of deliberative theology, we need to have a basic awareness of how theological positions and doctrines have emerged.

In this section, we turn to a brief overview of the eras of theological activity and theological movements that have shaped Christian belief and practice. We want to understand, in broad brushstrokes, how our thinking and teaching about God, our theological reflection, has developed over the course of Christian history and what questions have been of central concern. As you might imagine, a comprehensive treatment of the history of theological activity is well beyond the scope of this introductory volume, and we will only be able to sketch the basic contours of the development of theological thought, thus neglecting many significant developments. Our intent is not for you to understand the sweep of theological developments in great detail, but rather to learn how to read theologians in order to grasp their context and their major theological concerns or questions. What were the primary or driving concerns, broadly conceived, that theologians have taken up in each period and why? You should read this chapter with an eye for the big picture, which will enable you to return, in subsequent studies, to these theologians and eras with a framework for understanding in place.

Theology, Doctrine, and Dogma

Before we turn to the main questions raised in each era of theological inquiry, two related concerns need to be addressed that will clear a path forward. First, we need to distinguish among the terms *theology, doctrine*, and *dogma*. Second, it will be helpful to understand the underlying motivations for why Christians have constructed and reconstructed Christian doctrine down through the ages. These two discussions will enable us to navigate the broader sweep of theological movements and issues with greater clarity.

We have already defined theology as the study of God and the things of faith. Theology is an intellectual reflection upon the content of the Christian faith so that we might live out that faith in alignment with the scriptural witnesses, particularly those that bear witness to the way of Jesus Christ, who is the center of our faith. Theology, as this reasoned God-talk, is properly a task of the church. It is undertaken in order to strengthen and illuminate the life of faith. But it is crucial to grasp that theology is done by individuals on behalf of the larger church, and because theological reflection and writing is done by individuals, it may or may not rise to normative status within the church or a particular denomination. We will find many good examples of this distinction in the early church where questions about Jesus Christ, sin, worship, and other matters were debated by different theologians. Any one person's theological writing or position can be accepted or rejected by a community of faith. When rejected, that position does not disappear; it remains as a theological argument even though it falls short of providing guidance or a standard for the church's belief and practice. The key to keep in mind is that theology is an individual practice by those who wish to illuminate the life of faith or challenge prevailing perspectives and practices.

An individual theologian's reflection and articulation of Christian beliefs and practices can become part of the church's or a denomination's standard teachings through communal processes that affirm the meaningfulness and fittingness of that position. In the early church, ecumenical councils were the source of this affirmation. In today's Protestant denominations, various communal processes known as "polity" lead to or have in the past led to the acceptance of particular ways of understanding the Christian faith. These communally affirmed teachings are known as "dogma" or, more commonly today, "doctrine." The distinction between these two words is a bit ambiguous, but let's try to clarify the difference in contemporary usage.

The English word *dogma* comes from the Latin word meaning "principle" or "tenet," and through much of theological history, it referred to the authoritative teachings of the church. It is still used in the Catholic tradition to refer to beliefs and practices that have been confirmed as revealed by God and applicable to the faithful. Sometimes, the word *dogma* is used to connote a certain rigidity or inflexibility of thought, but in theological terms, it means something more akin to "authoritative." Generally speaking, the affirmation of theological positions as church dogma occurs through a hierarchical process in which those at the higher levels of authority—such as the pope—have a greater capacity to determine correct dogma than those lower in the hierarchy. In this sense, the theology of some individuals can take on normative status as a church dogma through a hierarchical process of affirmation.

Most Protestants today, however, speak of church doctrine, which is a word we have already used repeatedly in this introductory volume. Our English word *doctrine* comes originally from the Latin, meaning "teaching" or sometimes "learning," and refers to the teachings of the church that have been communally authorized. Church historian Jaroslav Pelikan defines it this way: "What the church of Jesus Christ believes, teaches, and confesses on the basis of the word of God: this is Christian doctrine."[1] For Protestant denominations today, the acceptance or affirmation of theology as sound doctrine tends to occur within democratic processes in which a larger body participates in determining the validity of doctrines. At the same time, we should recognize that the theological writings of the "founders" of different denominations are usually accorded a normative status for that community of believers. These "founding" doctrines could be altered by the larger community, but seldom, if ever, does this occur in practice, since the founders are considered to be authoritative in shaping the identity of the denomination. Thus, the writings of Calvin for Presbyterians and others in the Reformed tradition, those of Luther for the Lutherans, and Wesley's writings for Methodists have become doctrinal standards or normative for belief and practice within each of those communities of believers. At the same time, if Calvin, Luther, and Wesley were alive today, they might think the way we articulate and live out their teachings bears little resemblance to

 Make sure you can distinguish between theology and doctrine in their relationship to the church.

what they taught. We should note as well that in some nondenominational churches, the accepted doctrine or set of teachings may in fact be dependent upon a single person who leads the church, thereby conflating the individual's theology and the community's doctrine without a formalized process to affirm these teachings.

At this point, you might wish to pause and consider the church or denomination to which you belong (and in which you may feel called to full-time ministry). Do you have a sense of the doctrine, the standards, your community teaches and upholds? Do you know where to find those standards for belief and practice? If not, one place to start is at the denomination's or church's website, where a visitor usually can find information on the doctrines for the community and some sense of the theological origin of these communally held beliefs and practices. You may also wish to consider why it is important or common to maintain doctrinal standards. While there are different ways to answer this question, we can point to two primary considerations. First, doctrines form the basis of identity for any given community. They help us to know who we are as a community of believers, and at the same time, they help to distinguish our church from other churches or denominations. Second, for most churches and denominations, these doctrines are not abstract pronouncements, but rather, they say something important about our lived expression of the gospel. Doctrines indicate how we understand our calling to be disciples of Jesus Christ and to bear witness to our faith in the world. In other words, doctrines are much more than a set of beliefs to which we assent; they are the very core of our practice and embodiment of the Christian faith in specific times and places.

Many years ago, I received a call from a clergy colleague who lived in another state. He wanted some advice because he found himself in the midst of a raging controversy within his congregation. As he explained, he had been preaching a sermon series on "Who Is Jesus Christ?" and in the third and final sermon, he proclaimed from the pulpit about the humanity of Jesus. But in doing so, he stated that he believed Jesus was only a man and not divine. Following the service, many members of the congregation were upset with the pastor and even threatened to bring charges against him to church authorities. The colleague wanted me to affirm his sermon and denounce the narrow-mindedness of his congregation. Instead, I suggested that this clergy colleague had preached his own theology rather than the communally validated doctrines of the denomination. When he had been ordained in a denomination with a clear set of teachings that include the fully human and fully divine nature of Jesus Christ, this clergyperson had agreed to uphold and teach the community's beliefs and practices. When, instead, he offered up his own theology from the pulpit, church members were rightly upset.

The point here is that it is perfectly acceptable for a clergyperson or any church member to question and hold different theological positions, but when we represent the larger denomination or church community, we agree to teach and preach the doctrines that constitute our identity as Christians. When we are in the pulpit, we are not simply representing our own theology—which may be good theology or not so good theology—but are representing a long tradition of believers who have together discerned what we will teach, preach, and practice. Of course, sometimes a prophetic word must be proclaimed to break open systems, practices, and even doctrines that have turned away from God and toward human desires and brokenness. But prophetic practice, like any other theological activity, requires careful deliberation to avoid the pitfall of offering our own theology as God's word to the community.

Motivations for Doing Theology

With this sense of the difference between theology and doctrine, and in particular, the communally authorized nature of doctrine, we are now in a better position to consider the eras of theological activity and the theological movements that have shaped our contemporary understanding of the Christian faith. The practice of theology has enabled the continuous process of doctrinal development since the first Christians began to gather together.

But why? Why did early Christians feel it necessary to reflect upon their beliefs and practices? What was the motivation or impetus that spurred this process? In addition to the basic human drive to understand our existence, Maurice Wiles in his book *The Making of Christian Doctrine*, posits that three other primary motivations existed among the first theologians: apologetics, heresy, and clarification of the faith. Each of these has a particular concern or focal point that may or may not be particularly relevant in our contemporary setting.

By definition, apologetics means a defense of the faith against external opposition. The first Christians found themselves challenged to explain and defend their beliefs and practices to Jews and Greeks alike. Particularly pressing was the need to explain the one God who became flesh in Jesus of Nazareth and sent the Holy Spirit to be with believers. For strictly monotheistic Jews, this sounded like three gods. For polytheistic Greeks who had a panoply of gods for everything under the sun, including the sun (Helios), it made no sense to limit the gods to only three. Thus, early Christians began to articulate the doctrine of the Trinity, one God in three persons, which was affirmed by the Council of Nicaea in 325, thus granting it normative doctrinal status. Nevertheless, questions and criticism from non-Christians helped to move the early church to defend and thereby delineate this important doctrine. Today, there are theologians who continue to engage in apologetics, particularly seeking to explain and defend the faith in light of an increasingly secular and nonreligious or post-Christian society.

A second motivation for doctrinal development involved questions of heresy or the internal correction of false belief (in contrast to orthodoxy, which is, by definition, right belief or that which has been affirmed and authorized by the church). *Heresy* is not a word we often hear today in the Protestant context, largely because basic doctrines have been settled and denominationalism allows for varied interpretations of the basic doctrines. But there is an additional consideration related to the notion of heresy: sometimes orthodoxy, or what is thought to be good doctrine, may prove over time and by means of careful reflection to be out of step with the way of God and the scriptural witnesses. Sometimes prophetic voices are ultimately proven to be not heretics, but correctors of established beliefs, as is often demonstrated in the major and minor prophets of the Hebrew Scriptures, as well as by the witnesses to the prophet we know as Jesus of Nazareth.

Even so, in the early church, as doctrines were being articulated for the first time, debates arose that led to the determination of false belief. For example, Arius argued that Jesus Christ was not divine, but only the first or greatest among all creatures. This position was deemed heretical, as the fully divine nature of Christ was affirmed at the Council of Nicaea. Another example is the controversy in defining sin and grace, in which Pelagius argued that human beings can choose not to sin and do so unaided by grace. Augustine's articulation of the bondage of the will or our inability not to sin (in Latin, *non posse non peccare*) ultimately prevailed in favor of our utter reliance upon the grace of God. Despite this sense of "winners" and "losers" in the theological debates of the early church, we should keep in mind that those deemed heretics played a crucial role in helping the church think through what it believes and how it practices the faith. As Wiles emphasizes, "The influence of heresy on the early development of doctrine is so great that it is almost impossible to exaggerate it."[2]

The third motivation offered by Wiles is that of internal clarification of the faith among the believers. In every age, including our own, there are people who question and seek to understand Christian faith and teachings more deeply. These questioners lead us to reflect upon and clarify our teachings and practices. In the early church, of course, there were questions arising about every aspect of the faith, as churches formed and people

 Look back through the three basic motivations for the development of doctrine to make sure you understand each of them.

attempted to make sense of the Christian beliefs and practices, especially in light of the scriptural witnesses. A good contemporary example of this motivation for doctrinal development is found in the theology that arose following World War II and the horrors of the Holocaust. Christians found it impossible to ignore the question of where God was and how such evils could be perpetrated. These questions led theologians into a deeper consideration of the problem of evil, theodicy, in light of the nature of God and human free will. But we should be clear that this relatively recent theological reflection upon theodicy has not necessarily been affirmed by communal processes so as to rise to the level of doctrinal standard. Nonetheless, clarification of our Christian beliefs is an ongoing necessity because faith is a journey and never a destination.

Although apologetics, heresy, and internal clarification stand out as three primary motivations for doctrinal development, we can name additional reasons that might be closely related to these three. As noted earlier in this chapter, the impulse to interpret Scripture for the sake of Christian belief and practice has always been a primary one; thus, the importance of drawing out the meaning of the Bible can be seen as a hermeneutical or interpretive motivation. There is also the fact that our first-order discourse, the practices of the faith, especially in the early church, led to theological reflection and doctrinal development. For instance, the Eucharist, or Holy Communion, drew great criticism and charges of cannibalism in the early church, which believers were compelled to address in upholding that the bread is the body of Jesus and the wine is his blood. Pelikan also prevails upon us to grasp that, despite its central message of salvation, the early church had yet to discern the meaning and mechanism of salvation in Christ, thereby making the articulation of a doctrine of salvation, or soteriology, a primary focus in the first centuries following Christ's death and resurrection. Maybe, in your own mind, you can think of additional reasons for the ongoing development of doctrine as a necessary and helpful practice of the church.

All of these particular doctrinal considerations have continued to be discussed and developed through the history of the Christian faith, and while many denominations adhere to certain doctrinal standards, we should never view the process of reflecting upon and refining our teachings as closed and finished. As we turn next to a brief overview of the eras of theological activity and theological movements, we can note that certain teachings or particular questions predominate in different eras. For example, the rise of liberation theologies in the late 1960s and beyond led to an expanded understanding of the doctrine of sin (sometimes called hamartiology from the Greek word *harmatia*, "to miss the mark"). Liberation theologians have expanded our concept of sin by demonstrating not only its personal and individual form, but also the way sin is expressed in systems and institutions that are unjust. The language we use for the latter is "systemic sin." This development has deepened our understanding of the presence of sin in the world in significant ways, especially in light of our increasingly global and interconnected existence. We will have more to say about systemic sin in chapter 4. For now, as we proceed into the eras of theological activity, keep an eye turned to the broader brushstrokes of theology that arise in each period.

Periods of Theological Activity

With this overview of how and why doctrine develops, we can turn to considering some of the major questions and prominent theologians that have developed the church's teachings down through the centuries. Remember to think of theology as a stream flowing toward the ocean that is the fullness of God. Each human life enters this stream at a distinct point in time and within a particular lived context. When we see the movement of the stream over the centuries, we are better able to chart our own theological position or where we stand in this long stream of belief. The general periods of theological activity that we will address in a general fashion include the patristic era (c. 100–425 or, some suggest, 100–600), the medieval era or Middle Ages (c. 700–1300), the Reformation era (c. 1500–1750), the modern era (1750–c. 2000), and the so-called postmodern era in which we currently find ourselves. As you read about them, try to grasp the major points, themes, or questions that shaped each era, as well as the context in which the theologians of each era wrote. It should also be noted that the following overview relies upon the magisterial work of Jaroslav Pelikan, whose five-volume *History of Christian Doctrine* remains perhaps the most thorough treatment available of the church's doctrinal development.

The Patristic Era

The patristic era (sometimes called the period of the church "fathers") begins with the closing of the New Testament canon and continues through the Council of Nicaea in 325, though historians sometimes place the close of this era at the end of the seventh century. It is widely recognized as the period of theological activity that established some of the fundamental doctrines of the Christian faith: the two natures of Jesus Christ, the Trinity, grace and sin, as well as notions about the nature of the church. The Christian writers of this period, especially Augustine, have served as the basis for theological activity down through the ages, whether as a source of affirmation of the church's teachings or a point of critique. Nonetheless, the patristic era was the point of origin for the authority of what we know as "tradition," which is an important source for doing theology, as we will see in the next chapter. Remember that the tradition or communal affirmations enable the theology of individuals to become church doctrine. Another way to speak of this traditioning process is to consider the establishment of orthodoxy (literally, right teaching). In other words, the church began a process of affirming what is known, believed, taught, and confessed about Jesus Christ as the center or head or heart of the community of believers.

Several key doctrines were delineated during these early centuries, including the Trinity, the two natures of Jesus Christ, the holiness of the church, the nature of grace, the meaning of salvation, and the interpretation of Scripture. While each of these doctrines could be the subject of a chapter or even a book, at this point we will only sketch the basic contours of the discussions that unfolded. Our main concern is to recognize that, first, early theologians offered different understandings of the faith that were debated and settled but never without ongoing critique and reexamination, and second, that these basic considerations would be built upon in subsequent theological eras. Most significant for doctrinal development were the writings of Augustine, Bishop of Hippo, though Irenaeus, Tertullian, and even the "heretics" whose positions were defeated play a prominent role in clarifying and explaining what Christians believe.

One of the primary concerns of the early Christians, in light of the Jewish context from which Christian faith arose, was to articulate the importance of Jesus Christ and his relation to God. Judaism, of course, was expecting the Messiah, a brilliant political-military leader like King David who would restore the greatness of Israel. But this Messiah, Jesus Christ, brought new teachings, suffered and died on the cross, and rose again on the third day. Remember that there were external challenges requiring apologetics, challenges from those whose teachings would be deemed heretical or false, and internal discussions aimed at clarification of the faith. All of these converge in one primary question: Who is Jesus Christ? As a result, two central doctrines of the faith were established: the doctrine of the Trinity (one God in three persons) and the two natures of Jesus Christ (fully human and fully divine). We will consider these doctrines more closely in chapter 4. Key theologians who set the terms for these doctrinal statements included Tertullian, the Cappadocians, and Athanasius, and these teachings were confirmed by the Councils of Nicaea (325) and Chalcedon (451).

The second area of doctrinal development was what we refer to as ecclesiology, or the doctrine of the church. The church was a new entity and, therefore, as yet undefined. One of the early questions involved the holiness of the church, by which we mean that which makes it a community of restored and reconciled, though sinful, human beings. Baptism in the name of the Father, Son, and Holy Spirit was the entryway into the church's holiness, but in the midst of the persecution of the early church under Emperor Diocletian (reigned c. 303–305), a number of priests renounced Christianity and gave over sacred Christian texts to be burned. The question that was asked about these *traditores*, or those who handed over the faith (in contrast to those who faithfully hand it down), was whether the sacraments they had previously performed were valid, given that the one who had administered the rite had fallen away from the faith. The Donatists—a schismatic sect of Christians—argued for the rebaptism of those believers who had been baptized by *traditores*, in order to retain the purity of the church. The controversy continued throughout the fourth and into the fifth centuries. Augustine, Bishop of Hippo, responded most memorably to this challenge and concluded that the holiness of the church is never dependent upon the holiness or worthiness of the people, even the clergy. The office that represents God's grace, not the person, is where the holiness or authority is located. In other words, the validity of baptism lies in the action and holiness of God and only God. The phrase to represent this understanding of the church's sacraments and their efficacy is *ex opere operato* ("on account of the work which is done"), thereby suggesting the efficacy depends strictly upon the action of Christ in and through the sacrament. This position framed by Augustine has remained a basic tenet of the church's doctrine across the ages and still today. Augustine also argued that the schism of the Donatists was a graver error than the lapses of the persecuted.

Augustine also is credited for providing an initial understanding of sin and grace in his refutation of Pelagianism, which argued that human beings can choose not to sin. Augustine responded to this claim by arguing that we are not able not to sin (*non posse non peccare*) by means of our own will. As a result of this theological debate, doctrines related to original sin, the bondage of the will, the necessity of grace (and insufficiency of the law), and the importance of infant baptism took shape. In many respects, the manner in which Augustine framed the concepts of sin and grace continues to provide the basis for our understanding of these aspects of theological anthropology (the doctrine of the human being from a theological perspective), ecclesiology, and the doctrine of God. More will be said about the human condition as sinful but graced in chapter 4. Augustine's theology of grace became normative for Catholicism and within a number of Protestant traditions, though the question of infant baptism remains disputed among Protestants.

Let's read a brief extract from Augustine's treatise on "The Spirit and the Letter," which responds to Pelagius. Augustine writes:

> It is not our purpose in this work to expound the Epistle to the Romans, but to use its testimony to prove as surely as we may that the divine aid for the working of righteousness consists not in God's gift of the law, full as it is of good and holy commands, but in that our will itself, without which we cannot do the good, is aided and uplifted by the imparting of the Spirit of grace. Without that aid, the teaching is a letter that killeth.[3]

You may have just completed your first "close reading" of a primary theological text or, at least, a sliver of a text. In a close reading, we cannot skim the text, because it is so rich with meaning and intricate in its logic. It requires us to slow down and savor the writing. In fact, you might wish to read the excerpt a second time before continuing.

There are several things to note in our study of this brief excerpt. First, Augustine indicates that he is basing his theological case for the necessity of grace on the Scriptures and, in particular, Paul's letter to the Romans. Here we see that Augustine is telling us something about his sources or upon what grounds he makes his claim. Second, we read that both the law and grace are gifts of God, but that they must work in tandem, for without grace—which he equates with the Spirit—we cannot do what the law requires. Finally, notice that the title of the treatise, "The Spirit and the Letter," is reflected clearly in this passage as Augustine demonstrates the way that the Spirit of grace and the letter of the law operate in conjunction with the human will. Of course, if we were to read the entire treatise, the development of Augustine's full argument and logic would become clear. But this excerpt enables us to begin the process of reading theology as a spiritual practice. And when we read primary texts—the original writings of theologians—they may be difficult to understand and our reading slow and uncertain, but the depth of the wisdom contained within will often surprise us, move us, and open us to new ways of encountering the living God.

Two other doctrinal affirmations were articulated during the patristic period, though they will face ongoing discussion and reconstruction throughout the centuries to follow: (1) scriptural interpretation and its authority for the life of faith, and (2) the meaning of salvation in Christ. In the previous chapter, we addressed the two schools of thought related to scriptural interpretation, and this question of hermeneutics has been debated in all eras of theological activity. Clearly, the early church recognized the centrality of the scriptural witnesses as the primary source for theological and doctrinal affirmation. The problem, of course, has always been that texts can and have been read in various ways, suggesting a need for the church to also provide some standards for the validity of interpretations. Thus begins a question of the primacy of Scripture or tradition in the development of doctrines, which will come to a head during the Reformation.

The final development that deserves our attention in this brief overview is the meaning of salvation, or what we refer to as soteriology. Undoubtedly, the development of the church's understanding of Jesus Christ necessarily led to clarification of the meaning of salvation in Christ, with an emphasis on the establishment of a new creation and not simply the restoration of what was presumably lost in the fall. In many ways, soteriology (sometimes referred to as the work of Christ, in contrast to the person of Christ, or Christology) is the very heart of the Christian faith. It is in and through this Jesus who is the Christ and is himself God that human beings find the hope of life in its fullness, even life eternal. Of course, Christians will continue to explore the meaning of salvation throughout the centuries.

Indeed, as McGrath notes, virtually all the streams of Christian theology since the patristic era have been concerned with "continuing, extending, and, where necessary, criticizing the views of the early church writers."[4] As a result, the reflections of these first theologians have become official

 See if you can recall the key theological concerns of the patristic era. Consider the place of Augustine in these developments.

teachings of the church (i.e., doctrines) and normative for the church's belief and practice, even as they are continually refined and reformed. And with the affirmation of orthodoxy, the notion of tradition as a primary source for later theological reflection and doctrinal discernment is established.

The Medieval Era

At this point, we are able to turn toward the next major period of theological activity, the medieval period or the Middle Ages. It is important to note that the first major schism in church history occurred in 1054 with the separation of the Eastern and Western churches over theological differences. As a result, our overview of doctrinal development will proceed to trace the Western church, though we should recognize the rich theological tradition that will continue to develop among Eastern Orthodox churches. The medieval era, at least until the thirteenth century, is sometimes considered an intellectual low point in the development of the church's teachings. Pelikan refers to it as the "age of faith" in the sense of believing the church's teachings that were established in the patristic writings; in particular, Augustine's theology often prevails as the dominant voice.[5] Thus, it is suggested that the medieval era represents a fixing or consolidation of the patristic writings, more than the development of new theological concerns.

Several important institutions arose during this period and shaped the church's theology: monastic orders and the university. First, monastic and religious orders were formed during this period, and each order expressed a particular theology as the basis for its particular life together. Some of the most important monastic writings come from women such as Hildegard of Bingen, Catherine of Siena, and Julian of Norwich. Religious orders—in particular, the Franciscans, Dominicans, and Augustinians—participated in the academic study of theology as universities came into existence. Their central concerns were the role of reason (which then added a third source to the task of theology, alongside Scripture and tradition) and the systemization of the church's doctrines.

We have already mentioned the rise of scholasticism in relation to the development of theology as an academic discipline. The speculative divinity of scholasticism, with its impulse toward synthesizing Christian doctrine, providing for a reasoned justification of those teachings, and debating theological and philosophical questions, represented the essence of theological activity in this period. Peter Lombard's *Four Books of Sentences*, which systematized and wrestled with the contradictions and questions in the patristic teachings, especially those of Augustine, became the standard theological text studied in the medieval universities. But the height of the period is marked by Thomas Aquinas's *Summa Theologica*.

The following excerpt provides a sense of the form and content of Aquinas's theological and philosophical investigations:

Question 83: Of Free Will

Whether Man has Free-Will?

Objection I. It would seem that man has not free-will. For whoever has free-will does what he wills. But man does not what he wills, for it is written (Rom 7:19): *For the good which I will I do not, but the evil which I will not, that I do.* Therefore man has not free-will. . . .

I answer that, Man has free-will: otherwise counsels, exhortations, commands, prohibitions, rewards and punishments would be in vain. . . . Man acts from judgment, because by his apprehensive power he judges that something should be avoided or sought. But because this judgment, in the case of some particular act, is not from a natural instinct, but from some act of comparison in the reason, therefore he acts from free judgment . . . . And forasmuch as man is rational it is necessary that man have a free-will.[6]

Did you notice the pattern of Aquinas's theological argument, moving from objection (or the case against the stated question) to his answer, which addresses the initial objection? This short excerpt is typical of scholastic writings and should enable you to see more clearly how the exercise of reason and reasoned discourse became a primary source for theological engagement during the medieval era.

In sum, the questions of faith and reason and their relationship to each other were central concerns for medieval theology, as well as the development of a more comprehensive and systematic approach to or method of articulating what Christians believe and practice. Remember that through this era, there were essentially two streams of Christian thought: the Western church, which we would think of as Roman Catholicism, and the Eastern church or Eastern Orthodoxy. This twofold pattern of Christian

Pause again and put into your own words the characteristic theological concerns of the medieval era.

faith was soon to change radically as a result of deep theological differences among the faithful.

The Reformation

In the sixteenth century, the advent of the Reformation marks a turning point in theological development with the rise of doctrinal pluralism unlike that which had been seen in previous eras. Especially important was the rise of Protestant streams of theology, which would become the basis of distinct denominational doctrines. We will examine the key teachings of Luther and Calvin, including the fundamental claim to the authority of Scripture (*sola scriptura*, meaning "scripture alone") that stood in contrast to the growing emphasis on tradition within the Roman Catholic community. Perhaps the driving force behind the Reformation was this idea that Scripture should be the rule by which beliefs and practices are measured, and it is the only source necessary for theology. This position arises not only out of a response to scholasticism's speculative nature, but also in response to questionable practices present in the church, such as the abuses of indulgences, a practice intended for the remission of the penalty of sin. The Reformers, as Pelikan describes, were concerned primarily with "the 'wrong teaching' in the church, from which the 'wrong conduct' proceeded."[7]

Martin Luther's theology is definitive for the Reformation and provides us with a clear example of how the theological concerns of an individual become the concerns and, ultimately, the doctrinal affirmations of the community of faith. Today, of course, Luther's theology is normative for Lutheran communities of faith. Several theological concerns were at the forefront of Luther's teachings: justification by faith, the primacy of the Word in the life of the church, and the theology of the cross. Let's address each of these briefly.

First, Luther's emphasis on justification by faith or justification by grace through faith became the hallmark of Reformation thought. Justification is, of course, the forgiveness of sins, and the question for Luther was how someone can be forgiven by a righteous God. In the sixteenth century, forgiveness was generally offered by the priest through practices of penitence, indulgences, which could absolve the believer of the condemnation of sin. Luther questioned the validity and certainty of the forgiveness dispensed by human beings who are without righteousness by their own merit. Through his reading of Scripture, Luther concluded that the whole of the gospel is the message of justification by faith and the absolute need for God's grace. In contrast to what is known as "works-righteousness," or salvation through the accomplishing of good works, Luther stood firmly on the belief that salvation is possible only by the grace of God through the righteousness of Christ and can be received only by faith. All righteousness belongs to God. Even the justified believer remains a sinful creature, *simul justus et peccator* ("simultaneously justified and sinful"), with one foot in the new creation and the other planted in the old one. We should also note that Luther does not mean the kind of faith that is intellectual belief (*fides quae creditur*) or the knowledge of God's saving work, as was frequently the case in the medieval era, but rather, faith as an act of trust or confidence in Christ (*fides qua creditur*).

Let's pause here for another opportunity for close reading of a text, an excerpt from Martin Luther's "The Freedom of a Christian" (1520). As you read, try to follow his argument about justification by faith not works:

> Since, therefore, this faith can rule only in the inner man, as Rom. 10 [:10] says, "For man believes with his heart and so is justified," and since faith alone justifies, it is clear that the inner man cannot be justified, freed, or saved by any outer work or action at all, and that these works, whatever their character, have nothing to do with the inner man. On the other hand, only ungodliness and unbelief of heart, and no outer work, make him guilty and a damnable servant of sin. Wherefore it ought to be the first concern of every Christian to lay aside all confidence in works and increasingly to strengthen faith alone and through faith to grow in the knowledge, not of works, but of Christ Jesus, who suffered and rose for him, as Peter teaches in the last chapter of his first Epistle (1 Pet. 5:10). No other work makes a Christian.[8]

You probably found Luther's theology relatively easy to follow in this passage. He concludes that only the "work" of growing in faith in Jesus Christ can justify the human being, and that the act of faith leads to knowledge of the faith. Here he points to the heart of this doctrine of "faith alone" or, in Latin, *sola fide*. There is nothing the human being can do to save himself or herself. There is no means of forgiveness apart from faith in Christ. This is justification by faith. But notice that *sola fide* goes hand in hand with the teaching of *sola scriptura*, or "Scripture alone," as the source for theology. In the few sentences just quoted, Luther draws on Paul's letter to the Romans as well as 1 Peter. This referencing of Scripture is characteristic of Luther's writings.

The second doctrine central to Luther's teachings, then, is this emphasis on *sola scriptura*, or Scripture as the only valid authority for theological discernment. In the doctrine of justification by faith, the writings of Paul were Luther's primary authority or source material, though we should note that his interpretation of Paul has been subject to criticism over the centuries. Nonetheless, for Luther, the Bible contains all that is necessary for salvation. In a recent article, Hans Wiersma clarifies that *sola scriptura* does not mean the uncritical appropriation of the Bible. He argues that it is possible "to assert the principle of *Sola Scriptura* in a manner similar to the bumper sticker that says, 'The Bible Says It, I Believe It, That Settles It.' However, a Lutheran theological approach resists simplification. For Lutheran Christians, reading the Bible does not mean setting aside critical thinking skills."[9] Indeed, we can see in Luther's own writings a very careful and reasoned examination of Scripture. This emphasis on the authority of Scripture forms one of the basic commitments of the Reformation and Protestantism, and it stands in contrast to Roman Catholicism's affirmation of the tradition as authoritative for Christian teachings and for the discernment of the meaning of biblical texts.

The third teaching of Luther with which we should be familiar is known as the "theology of the cross" and suggests that Christ is known in his suffering. This doctrine, like that of justification by faith, arose out of his reading of Paul's letters in the New Testament. In contrast to the justification of works-righteousness, Luther held that human righteousness comes

---

 Describe the key theological contributions of Martin Luther, as discussed in this overview.

only by means of the cross of Jesus Christ: our sins are satisfied through his action vicariously on the cross. Moreover, the cross also represents the only access to an authentic knowledge of God and of salvation, though God remains hidden even as God is revealed in Christ. This theology of the cross articulated by Luther stands in contrast to the "theology of glory," a theology that stresses the human capacity to know God by means of reason and philosophical speculation, which he believed the scholastics espoused. Hence, for Luther, both knowledge of God and salvation are again utterly dependent upon faith and grace and upon the Word, which is Jesus Christ.

At this point, we turn to the second pivotal Reformation theologian, John Calvin, who also appealed directly to the authority of the Bible for his teachings. Today, of course, Calvin's theology has been affirmed by Reformed churches as normative doctrine. Calvin takes exception to the Lutheran concept of scriptural authority and suggests that the presence and will of God must also be embraced. Luther, in keeping with the Catholic heritage, affirmed the real, not symbolic, presence of God in the sacraments. By contrast, Calvin argued that in the sacraments, we find true representation (re-presentation), a spiritual but not physical presence of God. The Word is the means by which God's will may be known, and the sacraments confirm that will. Thus, for Calvin, in the Word and the sacraments working together, God is spiritually present. We see, then, that for Calvin's theology, the Bible is also a primary authority, but in conversation with the sacraments as the basis for confirming God's revealed yet hidden will.

Perhaps the most significant doctrinal development in Calvin's thought is what is known as "double predestination"—a position that Calvin found represented in the teachings of Augustine, as well as the Bible. While Luther taught only the belief in election to salvation, Calvin taught that God predestined some to salvation and others to damnation. This position is consistent with his emphasis on the sovereignty of God and the total depravity, or sinfulness, of the human creation. Calvin concluded that believers will place their trust in being among the elect to salvation, even though they may never know with certainty the actual will of God for their ultimate end. It is a way of saying that we choose to trust God above and before all else.

Once again, we turn to a close reading of a primary text, in this case, an excerpt from John Calvin's *Institutes* on the difficulties of the doctrine of election:

> If it is plain that it comes to pass by God's bidding that salvation is freely offered to some while others are barred from access to it, at once great and difficult questions spring up, explicable only when reverent minds regard as settled what they may suitably hold concerning election and predestination. A baffling question this seems to many. For they think nothing more inconsistent than that out of the common multitude of men some should be predestined to salvation, others to destruction. . . . We shall never be clearly persuaded, as we ought to be, that our salvation flows from the wellspring of God's free mercy until we come to know his eternal election, which illumines God's grace by this contrast: that he does not indiscriminately adopt all into the hope of salvation but gives to some what he denies to others.[10]

In wrestling with the doctrine of election and salvation, especially the notion that God chooses some for damnation, are you able to grasp the theological and spiritual basis for Calvin's claim? Calvin places all grace, all mercy, all sovereignty, all will to determine salvation in the hands of God. Whether or not we believe in predestination and, particularly, double predestination, we can still grasp the power of throwing ourselves utterly and entirely upon God's mercy and of choosing to love God and follow Christ whether or not we are chosen for salvation. That is a demonstrable act of faith.

The followers of Calvin continued to develop his teachings on double predestination and God's will as keys to the Christian life. At the Synod of Dort (1618–1619), which was held among the Dutch Reformed churches to dispute the rise of Arminianism (a theology of grace), the Calvinist

---

 Note the differences between Calvin's and Luther's theology. Describe, in your own words, the doctrine of double predestination.

---

doctrinal position was reinforced and became normative. Today, we often use the acronym TULIP to represent the key teachings or five points of Calvinism: Total depravity, Unconditional election, Limited atonement, Irresistible grace, and Perseverance of the saints or the elect to salvation.

The followers of theologian Jacob Arminius, known as the Remonstrants, objected to the predestinarianism of Calvin, arguing that God's will in Christ is for universal salvation, for all to be saved through faith in Christ. Although this Arminian position was rejected at the Synod of Dort, as we will soon see, it became a central teaching in the rise of Methodism in the eighteenth century.

While our account of the teachings of the Christian faith henceforth is concerned with the Protestant stream of doctrine, we do well to note that Roman Catholicism responded to the Reformation and its criticisms at the Council of Trent (1545–1563). There the Roman Catholic Church would clarify doctrines and affirm the importance of the apostolic succession in handing down the truth of the gospel from generation to generation, thus placing authority for the church's teachings in the tradition as much as in the Scriptures. Like the Reformers, the theologians of the Catholic Counter-Reformation would turn to Augustine's writings and find support for their emphasis on the primacy of the church or tradition. By now we should begin to see that both the Bible and the early Christian theologians can be interpreted in various ways. Some streams of the Christian faith will claim to be the only true interpretation, while most Christians today recognize that there are varieties of faithful interpretations and expressions of the Christian faith down through the ages. Those who seek the one true way of following Christ will sometimes become so rigid in their thinking as to miss the movement of the Spirit and the presence of God in the world.

Before turning to the modern era and its wealth of theological activity, we want to mention one other theological stream that arose during the Reformation: Anabaptism. Although the source of its development remains disputed—no one can say with certainty where and how it came to be— the primary teaching was the rejection of infant baptism and the need to rebaptize in a believers' baptism. This was, of course, a radical break from the institutional church. While some might think that today's Anabaptists are found in various threads of the Baptist churches, in fact, Anabaptism is continued among Christian groups such as the Amish, Moravians, and Hutterites. Anabaptists are sometimes called the Radical Reformers because their doctrines seek to uphold an extreme biblical purity.

This brings us to a brief summary of the Reformation era. What would you think, at this point, are some of the major teachings that arose during this period? If you pointed to the notion of *sola scriptura* and the authority of the Bible for the church's doctrine, that would be a sound response. If you named the rise of doctrinal pluralism—the varieties of teachings now dotting the Christian landscape—that, too, would be a good answer. Perhaps you named the emphasis on justification by faith. We have also noted the emergence of new ways of expressing the meaning of salvation in Christ and the significance of God's will for the faithful. Yet, even as the Reformers introduced new doctrines, we should not miss the continuity with the church teachings that had been developed in earlier eras: the importance of the person of Jesus Christ and the Trinity remained central to Reformation teachings, as did a reliance on the writings of the patristic era (though, admittedly, they can be read to support different positions, as with the Bible). Finally, of course, while the Reformation theologians did not reject entirely the authority of the church as the source for the normativity of doctrines, they did stand in contrast to the teachings of Roman Catholicism by privileging the Word of God in the Bible as their primary source. The privileged place of Scripture also led the Protestant churches (with the exception of those in the Anglican tradition) to confirm only two sacraments—baptism and Holy Communion—in distinction from the seven found in Roman Catholicism. These doctrines that emerged in the Protestant Reformation would continue to undergo refinement and further development in the centuries that follow.

The Modern Era

At this point, we turn to the modern era of theological and doctrinal activity. Intellectually and theologically, a distinct shift occurs due to the rise of Enlightenment thought. To grasp the contours of the modern era, we need to become familiar with three key thinkers and the basic assumptions or mind-set that shaped this period of theological activity. In many ways, you and I today have been profoundly shaped by the Enlightenment, even if we are not conscious of that influence. Though many philosophers were instrumental in articulating the ideas and the spirit of the modern era, three will help us grasp its basic framework: René Descartes, David Hume, and Immanuel Kant.

The French mathematician, scientist, and philosopher René Descartes (1596–1650) was among the first thinkers to engage what would become fundamental concepts of the Enlightenment and modernity. He is best remembered for the phrase *cogito ergo sum*, which translates, "I think, therefore I am." This phrase might be considered shorthand for the rise of reason as the primary source for discovering truth and knowledge. Descartes would suggest that our capacity to think and reason does not depend upon sense experience or the physical world. In addition, Descartes' philosophy might also be considered the genesis of the turn to the individual and individual autonomy, which would culminate in the individualism of late modernity.

The Scottish philosopher David Hume (1711–1776) likewise investigated questions of epistemology (the study of knowledge) and argued that the basis for philosophy (or theology, for that matter) should be observation and fact, rather than "superstition." For Hume and others, religious authorities would be included among the superstitious, which is a skepticism often expressed in contemporary society. Hume's *Natural History of Religions* (1757) is generally considered to be the first empirical (i.e., derived from observation) study of religion, arguing for a developmental or evolutionary model in which polytheistic religions are inferior to the later and more advanced monotheistic religions (though Hume would also suggest that polytheistic religions are more tolerant than monotheistic ones). Thus, in Hume's work, we see the importance of a rational and empirical consideration of faith, as well as a sense of progress or steady improvement over time.

The height of Enlightenment thought is found in the writings of the most influential thinker of the modern period, the German philosopher Immanuel Kant (1724–1804). Kant built upon the philosophy of Descartes, Hume, and others in three important "Critiques" (i.e., reasoned investigations of what can be known apart from experience). In these three major works, he asks: (1) What can we know? (*Critique of Pure Reason*); 2) What ought we do? (*Critique of Practical Reason*); and 3) What may we hope? (*Critique of Judgment*). Significantly, Kant suggested that human reason alone and apart from any reference to God or experience provides us with the basis for making moral judgments. We do not need the beliefs of Christian faith or the supposed rewards and punishment of God in order to know how we should live and what we should do. Kant's point was not to deny the existence of God (as later interpreters of Kant would contend), but rather to advance the notion that human beings would have the capacity to make moral choices even if God did not exist. Thus, in Kant, reason becomes the central human attribute that enables us to pursue moral perfection. We should also note Kant's emphasis upon the capacities of the human being apart from relying on the grace or will of God.

There are, of course, countless other philosophers, scientists, and writers who shaped the Enlightenment and modernity—far too many to mention in this brief introduction. Most relevant for our discussion here are the basic precepts or mind-set that took hold during the modern era. We can point to several key ideas that shaped the modern sensibilities and directly influenced the theological works that were produced. Different authors have named or organized these ideas in different ways, but they point toward the same general set of intellectual assumptions. First, modernity held an optimistic view of human potential. Second, there was a suspicion of tra-

 Read back through the basic assumptions of the modern era, and try to articulate them in your own words.

ditional authorities, including the church. Third, modernity emphasized reason and, more importantly, the autonomous rational self or individual who could make judgments apart from those authorities. Fourth, there was also a belief in progress or perfectibility through science and technology, through fact and observation, toward a utopian future. Fifth, in modernity, faith and religion became "private" matters as opposed to "public" concerns. As we will soon see, these modern assumptions shaped the theological activity of the period, as they were incorporated into theological proposals by some and critiqued by others.

As we examine a few key theologians representative of the modern era, we should keep in mind not only the distinct mind-set of modernity, but also that, on the heels of the Reformation, there were now a wide variety of theological positions, though few of these theologies would become doctrinal standards. One clear exception was the theology of John Wesley, which would eventually be affirmed as the basic doctrinal standards for Methodism. So we begin with a brief word on the theology of Wesley, who lived at the cusp of the Enlightenment. Then we will briefly examine the following key theologians and theological movements: Schleiermacher, Kierkegaard, Barth, Tillich, Bonhoeffer, liberation theologies, and what we will refer to here under the general rubric of "relational" theologies. But first, let's turn our attention to another major denominational "founder," John Wesley, and his theology.

John Wesley (1703–1791) began a renewal movement within the Church of England that was "evangelical" in the eighteenth-century use of the word to mean experiential. For Wesley, the church was going through the motions; it had the form of religion, but not the spirituality, devotion, or experience of God. Though his writings are not systematic and his theology is primarily articulated in sermons, Wesley's theology has become normative for those in the broader Methodist tradition. Remember that at the Synod of Dort, the followers of Jacob Arminius argued against the Calvinist position, which prevailed. Yet the Arminian position endured. Decades later, Wesley developed and applied the theology of grace espoused by Arminius and his followers, the Remonstrants. In contrast to the Calvinist position represented by the acronym TULIP, Wesley taught that (1) although human beings are totally depraved or sinful, they are also preveniently graced; (2) election is conditional only in the sense that people must choose to accept God's freely offered grace; (3) atonement is unlimited, in that Christ died for all; (4) God's grace is resistible; and (5) those who continue to rely on grace have the assurance of their salvation. Wesley's theology thus suggested a divine-human synergism in which salvation is a lifelong process by which, through reliance on the grace of God, we may be perfected in love or sanctified. Wesley also drew upon the experience of God in the life of the believer as a source for his theology, in addition to the existing triad of Scripture, tradition, and reason, though Wesley held Scripture to be primary, in continuity with the Reformation emphasis on *sola scriptura*. We should note that, in keeping with the onset of Enlightenment thought, Wesley took the science of his day quite seriously, though never at the sacrifice of the sovereignty and work of God in the world. Indeed, on the question of God's sovereignty, Wesley would claim to be only a "hair's breadth" away from Calvin.

At this point, we can examine a few of the theologians who were shaped by and, in turn, shaped the modern mind-set, beginning with the German theologian Friedrich Schleiermacher (1768–1834). Schleiermacher was a Reformed theologian and is often considered the father of liberal Protestantism, since his theological writings provide the basic conceptual framework for theological liberalism. Writing during the rise of Romanticism— a movement that reacted against the captivity to reason and empiricism

As you read about the "relational" theologies, it may be helpful to use the following matrix to jot down the key ideas of these modern theologians, in order to compare and contrast their theologies.

Matrix of Modern Theologians

Theologian	Movement	Time Frame	Context	Starting Point	Influences
Schleiermacher					
Kierkegaard					
Barth					
Bonhoeffer					
Tillich					
Cone					
McFague					

during the late eighteenth and early nineteenth centuries—Schleiermacher addressed the "cultured despisers" of his day (think: apologetics) and sought to make the Christian faith relevant by appealing to "feeling" or knowing God affectively, not simply intellectually. In his major work, *The Christian Faith*, Schleiermacher defined religion in terms of a "feeling of absolute dependence," a sense of and taste for the infinite, or a sort of God-consciousness. In Schleiermacher, we find an important turn to the individual's engagement with the infinite, as well as a desire to make the Christian faith meaningful in light of the culture in which it existed. In Schleiermacher, the individual human being comes to the forefront as an entry point for theological reflection.

Today, in the twenty-first century, the word *liberal* is widely used and, in relation to theology, generally misused and misunderstood. Classic theological liberalism, as inspired by Schleiermacher, has several distinct dimensions that arose in response to the Enlightenment. Classic liberalism is characterized by an optimism in the human potential, through reason and experience, to interpret scripture and know the divine apart from traditional authorities. In addition, there is an intentional engagement of the culture and common human experience that suggests Christian faith

---

 Briefly describe the meaning of "classical theological liberalism" or "liberal Protestantism," as it is sometimes called.

---

need not be opposed to cultural forms but can be expressed within them. Liberalism tends to utilize historical-critical methods of interpretation, taking scientific knowledge seriously, and accepts the premise that we possess the capacity to make moral judgments—and thereby make progress toward the greater good—without dependence upon the commandments or will of God. Of course, variations on these themes are many, and what is considered "liberal" inevitably depends upon one's perspective. Nonetheless, when speaking of theological liberalism, we should recognize the meaning and contours of classic liberalism.

In Denmark, Søren Kierkegaard (1813–1855), who is a product of the Lutheran tradition, also emphasized the individual and experience in his theological and philosophical writings. Usually, we refer to his theology as "existentialism," in which a person's salvation or damnation depends greatly upon individual choices. Existentialists grant that human beings have a significant measure of freedom to act and to create their lives. This responsibility results in a situation of "angst," or anxiety as we experience the dread or fear associated with having the freedom to choose and, quite possibly, to choose wrongly. The religious life, governed by faith in God and allowing for the suspension of reason, is the highest form of existence and includes a personal and subjective experience of God. For Kierkegaard, faith and religion, as the pursuit of spiritual development, are largely a personal, individual process. It is Kierkegaard who first regards faith as a "leap" or a suspension of reason in pursuit of the divine, and in his theological writings, the human being and our human condition of anxiety serve as the starting point for theological reflection. Kierkegaard's existentialism shaped and influenced a number of theologians and theological proposals throughout the modern era.

Of course, there was considerably more theological activity in the nineteenth century, but at this point, we transition into the twentieth century and the rise of neo-orthodoxy, a movement associated with the Swiss Reformed theologian Karl Barth (1886–1968), who published *The Epistle to the Romans* (in German, *Der Römerbrief*) in 1919. This landmark statement, the opening to a long theological career, was a direct response to the classic liberalism of his day, especially in light of the horrors of World War I, which cast doubt on the liberal optimism of human freedom and progress toward a better world. Barth rejects the starting point of the human being and begins instead with the wholly other or transcendent God, utterly unknowable and unapproachable apart from Jesus Christ, who is the mediator between God and humanity. The self-revelation of the Word of God also figures prominently in Barth's theology as a threefold word of Jesus Christ, Scripture, and the church's proclamation. Barth's unfinished major theological work, *Church Dogmatics*, best illustrates his "lifelong search . . . to establish a strong position for orthodox Christian faith in a world in which it had been marginalized."[11]

Barth, then, is associated with the movement known as neo-orthodoxy (*neo* meaning new or recent, and *orthodoxy* literally meaning right teaching), which rejected the nineteenth century's turn to culture and the human potential and sought to restore Reformation teachings in large measure. Yet, given the insights of the Enlightenment and the modern mind-set, neo-orthodoxy was a reinterpretation of earlier teachings. Barth accepted scientific and historical methods and knowledge, as well as the relevance of the gospel message to the realities of the world, even though he rejected the liberal optimism in the human potential and sought to reclaim an utter dependence upon God and the cross of Jesus Christ.

In Germany, during the rise of National Socialism, Dietrich Bonhoeffer (1906–1945), whose theological roots lay in Lutheranism, crafted a unique theological statement that resists easy categorization, especially since his life and theological career were cut short due to his participation in the German resistance in World War II. Bonhoeffer has been appreciated by more traditional communities and more progressive ones alike, but for different dimensions of his theology. On the one hand, Bonhoeffer's *Life Together* and *The Cost of Discipleship* offer a rather traditional and scriptural approach to theological reflection, which is deeply meaningful and insightful. Bonhoeffer's theology is concerned with the church, the Christian life, and the meaning of Jesus Christ. Yet Bonhoeffer is also known for unusual and fragmentary theological concerns, largely found in his writings while imprisoned, which have been the source of great debate. Some suggest that his notion of "religionless Christianity" serves to emphasize faith rather than institutional religion and that Bonhoeffer envisioned the end of the church as institution. Bonhoeffer displayed an openness to other religions in his concern for Judaism and the Old Testament, as well as his expressed desire to travel to India to meet Gandhi and find "Christ" in the East. Bonhoeffer's last work, unfinished at the time of his death, was a manuscript on ethics, leading some to propose that a mature Bonhoeffer might have been an ethicist more than a theologian. In sum, Bonhoeffer remains something of an enigma, difficult to locate within a theological movement. Perhaps his theology represents a transitional project leading from liberalism and neo-orthodoxy toward liberation theologies. Unfortunately, we will never know what Bonhoeffer might have become and written had he lived into his forties and beyond.

A second product of the tragic realities of World War II was the German Lutheran theologian Paul Tillich (1886–1965), who spent the better part of his theological career in the United States. Tillich's three-volume *Systematic Theology* displays both classic liberal and existential concerns, and his "method of correlation" sought to answer the philosophical questions of the culture by means of the theological message of the gospel. This correlation of culture and Christian faith continued the liberal concern for speaking meaningfully to the contemporary culture. Tillich also wrote of the anxiety of potential non-being in light of the horrors witnessed in the world. A product of the 1950s and 1960s, Tillich engaged the symbols and insights of depth psychology, as well as numerous philosophical and theological predecessors, to create a rich and intricate theological system. Existentially, in light of the anxious question of the possibility of non-being, Tillich proposed the answer present in the Christian message of "Being Itself," or God as our "ultimate concern." The question of "estrangement," which is Tillich's symbol for sin, is answered by the Christian symbol of the New Being in Jesus as the Christ. The fragmentation and ambiguity of existence are answered by the Christian message of the divine Spirit by which we are grasped into a state of unity and unambiguous life. Tillich's theology was widely influential in the 1960s and 1970s and continues to be an important source for contemporary theologians.

In 1969, amid the tumult of the civil rights movement, protests over the Vietnam War, the end of colonialism, and other dramatic events, a new theological movement was initiated with the publication of *Black Theology and Black Power* by James Cone (b. 1938). In Latin America, the Peruvian Catholic theologian Gustavo Gutiérrez (b. 1928) was simultaneously at work on a "theology of liberation," though it would not be published in English until 1973 (in Spanish, it appeared in 1971). As a result, in North America, Cone's theology was the first major work of liberation theology widely available. Cone was concerned with the question of how one can be Black and Christian, given the ways in which Christian religion has been used to dehumanize and oppress African Americans in direct contradiction to the gospel of Jesus Christ. Thus, Cone argues that the scriptural witnesses demonstrate that God is on the side of the oppressed and marginalized, and the liberation of those who are oppressed is at the heart of the gospel.

A multitude of liberation theologies have since emerged, not only in the Americas, but around the globe, including feminist, Womanist, Latino, Mujerista, Asian, African, Dalit, and many others. Liberation theologies not only claim the starting point of God's preferential option for the poor, marginalized, and powerless, but also express a concern for justice as essential to any theological statement. One of the most important contributions of liberation theologies has been the introduction of the concept of systemic sin, which suggests that there are systems and structures, institutional arrangements, that perpetrate and perpetuate sin and that we participate knowingly and unknowingly in those sinful systems, thereby making us complicit. We will return to the concept of systemic sin in chapter 4. Significantly, liberation theologies challenged the notion of any theological statement being "neutral" or context-free and therefore universally valid—a consideration we will examine more carefully in the next chapter.

Finally, in more recent years, a variety of theological proposals have appeared on the landscape that we might refer to more broadly as relational theologies, due to their emphasis on or starting point in the notion of the interrelatedness of all of existence with the divine. We might include process theologies, economic theologies, and ecological theologies in this broadly conceived theological movement, which responds to concerns of the late twentieth century, including globalism, inequality, and the problem of evil. One example of a relational theology is the ecological theology of Sallie McFague (b. 1933), which can be viewed as an outgrowth of her earlier work in feminist liberation theology, with its expansion toward a concern for the liberation of the whole of creation and not just people. McFague's *The Body of God: An Ecological Theology* introduced the metaphor of God's body as a way of referring to the world and the need to liberate a burdened and suffering creation. Her basic premise is that "all beings and processes on the planet, are interrelated, and that the well-being of each is connected to the well-being of the whole."[12] This sense of the interwoven relationships of all living things with each other and God leads to a basic premise: that salvation, healing and wholeness, is not only a human concern but a cosmic one. Relational theologies, of course, represent a wide and varied group of theological writings and concerns, but McFague's proposal enables us to grasp the centrality of relationality in these projects, despite their differences.

One final theological movement worth mentioning is evangelical theology in the modern period. Evangelicalism was initially related to the Reformation and, as we have seen, was associated with the rise of Methodism in England in the eighteenth century. In earlier times, and in other languages such as Spanish and German, *evangelical* has been used synonymously with *Protestant*. However, in the twentieth century and beyond, the meaning of evangelical has shifted to reflect a theological position generally associated with a basic pattern of beliefs, described by historian Mark Noll to include: (1) conversion, (2) the Bible as containing all spiritual truth, (3) a concern

Familiarize yourself with the meaning of *evangelical* as defined by Noll, and compare it with the eighteenth-century usage.

for evangelism and mission, and (4) the centrality of the cross in providing for the atonement of sin and salvation.[13] While evangelicals are often found among nondenominational churches, the movement crosses over denominational lines and is present in various institutional and theological expressions.

The Postmodern Era

Before concluding our brief account of the periods of theological activity, we should acknowledge the shift that has occurred in recent decades, in which the basic assumptions of modernity are being challenged. The confidence in the human potential and reason, including the capacity of science and technology to solve all our problems, has eroded. The height of individualism and the subsequent loss of many forms of community has been called into question. Thus, we find ourselves at the cusp of a new period of intellectual and theological history, often referred to as the postmodern era. Postmodernity is best characterized by reference to the unraveling of the modern assumptions; however, the shape of the new intellectual milieu, in a positive or constructive sense, has not yet come into clear focus. Perhaps the Millennial Generation, sometimes referred to as "digital natives," will provide us with the great theological works born out of the postmodern worldview.

Regrettably, our brief overview of theological activity across the centuries has omitted many significant theological voices and could certainly be critiqued for this reason. But our purpose has not been to provide a comprehensive account of all theologians and theological movements, but rather to provide an awareness of the streams of theological engagement and to encourage you to begin sorting through the various positions, so that you might discern where your own theological positions have their roots and find their energy. When we are reading a particular theologian, it is always helpful to ask questions about the context, time frame, starting point, and prior influences that shape and ground the theological project. These considerations help us to better understand the perspective from which he or she writes, whether or not we agree with that theological position. This is an important reminder: whenever we study theology, our goal is to hear one another with open minds and hearts and to seek understanding, even if we do not agree.

Before the conclusion of this chapter, one last piece of information will also help you engage in future theological study. At several points, this

 Be sure that you understand the difference between primary and secondary texts.

chapter offered short excerpts from various theologians so that you might read and interpret them for yourself. Whenever we read the actual writings of a theologian, we are engaging primary texts or sources. These original writings may be somewhat difficult reading, but the fact that they continue to endure over decades and centuries tells us that they contain significant insights for the Christian faith. In contrast, if we read a book about someone's theology—for example, an interpretation of Karl Barth's *Epistle to the Romans* or an overview of Augustine's *City of God*—we are engaging secondary texts or sources. The best way to know and understand any theologian is to read the primary sources yourself, but secondary sources can help you wrestle with and make sense of those texts.

So, then, how would you categorize this short introduction you are reading now? Of course, this is a secondary source, which provides you with a limited and basic overview of many theologians and doctrines. But its goal is to provide you with a taste for theology and a road map for navigating the discipline, so you will be encouraged and able to read theology and primary texts in the future. If you are ready to go a little deeper still, then the next chapter will introduce you to how we do theology, its methods and sources.

Questions for Personal Exploration

1. Can you think of a time when you heard a sermon or participated in a class where someone neglected to distinguish his or her own theology from the church community's doctrines? How do you feel about a preacher presenting his or her own theological views in a sermon?

2. We explored some of the motivations for the development of doctrine over time. Which motivations do you think are most evident in the contemporary period, and why?
3. Skim back through the eras of theological activity. What are the theological debates or doctrines that you found most surprising or most unlike your own beliefs? Do you think some theological eras were more important than others for the development of the church's teachings?
4. How would you describe the "close reading" of a theological text? Is there a process you would use or something you might do to assist your comprehension of the text?

Resources for Deeper Exploration

A good theological dictionary or encyclopedia of theology will provide you with an introduction to most of the important theological figures and debates through which doctrine has developed.

Blackwell Publishing, for instance, has produced a series of volumes introducing the theology of each of the Christian eras, beginning with *The First Christian Theologians*, edited by G. R. Evans (Malden, MA: Blackwell, 2004).

Pelikan, Jaroslav. *The Christian Tradition: A History of the Development of Doctrine.* 5 vols. Chicago: University of Chicago Press. While difficult reading, each of the five volumes contains a wealth of information about the history of doctrinal development.

Wiles, Maurice. *The Making of Christian Doctrine.* Cambridge: Cambridge University Press, 1967.

Notes

1. Jaroslav Pelikan, *The Christian Tradition: A History of the Development of Doctrine,* vol. 1, *The Emergence of the Catholic Tradition (100–600)* (Chicago: University of Chicago Press, 1971), 1.

2. Maurice Wiles, *The Making of Christian Doctrine* (Cambridge: Cambridge University Press, 1967), 36.

3. John Burnaby, ed. and trans., *Augustine: Later Works* (Philadelphia: Westminster, 1955), 209.

4. Alister E. McGrath, *Christian Theology: An Introduction,* 4th ed. (Malden, MA: Blackwell, 2007), 7.

5. Jaroslav Pelikan, *The Christian Tradition: A History of the Development of Doctrine*, vol. 3, *The Growth of Medieval Theology (600–1300)* (Chicago: University of Chicago Press, 1978), 4, 50.

6. Peter Kreeft, ed., *A Shorter Summa: The Essential Philosophical Passages of St. Thomas Aquinas' Summa Theologica* (San Francisco: Ignatius, 1993), 111.

7. Pelikan, *Reformation of Church and Dogma (1300-1700)*, vol. 4 (Chicago: University of Chicago Press, 1984), 247.

8. Martin Luther, "The Freedom of a Christian," in *Martin Luther's Basic Theological Writings*, ed. Timothy F. Lull (Minneapolis: Fortress Press, 1989), 599.

9. Hans Wiersma, "A Brief Introduction to *sola scriptura*," *Lutheran Theology: An Online Journal*, January 18, 2011, http://lutherantheology.wordpress.com/2011/01/18/a-brief-introduction-to-sola-scriptura/.

10. John Calvin, *Calvin's Institutes: A New Compend*, ed. Hugh T. Kerr (Louisville: Westminster John Knox, 1989), 113.

11. Daniel W. Hardy, "Karl Barth," in *The Modern Theologians*, ed. David F. Ford (Malden, MA: Blackwell, 2005), 36.

12. Sallie McFague, *The Body of God: An Ecological Theology* (Minneapolis: Augsburg Fortress, 1993), 8.

13. Mark A. Noll, *The Rise of Evangelicalism: The Age of Edwards, Whitefield, and the Wesleys* (Downers Grove, IL: InterVarsity, 2003), 19. Noll relies upon the work of David W. Bebbington, *Evangelicalism in Modern Britain: A History from the 1730s to the 1980s* (London: Unwin Hyman, 1989).

Chapter 3

How Do We Do Theology?

In the first two chapters, we considered two primary questions: What is theology? And how has theology developed over the centuries? Now in chapter 3, we turn to the question of how we do theology. This question points us to prolegomena (literally, "things said before"), the preliminaries that enable us to make careful and deliberative claims about God and the life of faith. We refer to these concerns that shape how we do theology as theological method. Because theology is fundamentally related to language and the careful use of language to express the things unseen, our preliminary considerations begin with how language about God functions and should be engaged. Once we have some facility with theological language, our study of prolegomena then considers the norm for doing theology—the standard or yardstick—against which our claims should be measured. We will examine the sources for doing theology: Scripture, tradition, reason, and experience, as well as mention newer sources that have been introduced in recent decades and the question of culture or context for doing theology. Finally, this chapter concludes with a brief consideration of how different theological projects will demonstrate different orienting concerns or starting points. Identifying the central concern can help us to read theology with greater comprehension.

Theological Language

Our only way to share who God is and the life of faith is by means of language. It is a unique gift given to human beings. Suggesting that language is the only way to share our faith in God does not imply that we cannot bear witness with our lives and actions or that we cannot experience the reality of God. But it does indicate that language provides us with access to God in a way that is uniquely important to the life of faith. The book of Genesis tells us that God created by speaking the cosmos into existence, declaring it to be good. We recognize that God gave human beings the Word become flesh, Jesus Christ, and the words of Scripture to enable us to know God more fully, though never completely. Our use of language can limit how God is known in our lives and communities of faith, or it can express the infinite, wondrous, elusive, immense reality of God and encourage us to know the divine more deeply. In this section, we will begin by considering how easy it is to limit the word and revelation of God by the paucity of our own human words. By doing so, we will then be better able to grasp how expansive and even poetic language opens us to a deeper and wider knowledge of who God is and what God intends for the world.

Let's begin by considering the language you normally use to refer to God. If you are like many church members, you have often heard God spoken of as "Father" and have adopted this as the appropriate way to refer to God. Of course, the early church did use the language of Father, as did Jesus in speaking of *Abba* (an expression of intimacy), but there is far more to consider before drawing any conclusions about its correctness. When we speak of God as "Father," we are using a metaphor in which we speak of one thing in terms of another. We are saying, "God *is like* a

 Define metaphor in your own words, and be sure you understand how it functions.

father." But every metaphor breaks down at some point, and we encounter the opposite: "God *is not like* a father." It might be helpful to think for a moment about the ways God can be considered father-like: we believe our life comes from God; God cares for us like a parent; God disciplines and loves us alike. Now think about the ways God is not like a father: God does not have a physical body and is not biologically male; some people have terrible fathers who would not enable them to think positively about God; God does not fall short the way even the best fathers do. In addition, the way Aramaic speakers in first-century Palestine would have understood *Abba* no doubt differs considerably from our twenty-first-century usage in North America of *father*. So if the only way we refer to God is as a father, we are severely restricting our understanding of who God is and how God relates to the world.

The use of metaphor is actually the only means we have to speak of God. We cannot describe God directly, because God is Spirit, not a physical person. We can describe a table, an animal, an ocean shore, or another person using direct descriptors, but this simply is not the case for the divine. We find a multitude of metaphors in the Scriptures, as the biblical writers and Jesus attempt to explain, honor, and name God. If we turn to Psalm 62, we encounter a good example of an abundance of metaphors in one short text. Read carefully through verses 5-9 of the psalm, and see how many metaphors you can identify:

> For God alone my soul waits in silence,
>   for my hope is from him.
> He alone is my rock and my salvation,
>   my fortress; I shall not be shaken.
> On God rests my deliverance and my honor;
>   my mighty rock, my refuge is in God.
>
> Trust in him at all times, O people;
> pour out your heart before him;
>   God is a refuge for us.
>
> Those of low estate are but a breath,
>   those of high estate are a delusion;
>   in the balances they go up;
>   they are together lighter than a breath.

What are some of the metaphors for God in these verses? If you pointed to "fortress," "rock," and "refuge," you would be right. Sometimes a perceptive student will point to the word "he" for God and suggest that this

Once you are familiar with the metaphors in this excerpt from Psalm 62, read another psalm and try to identify the metaphors at work.

pronoun, too, is metaphorical, since God is neither male nor female. But there are other metaphors at work in this psalm. The phrase "pour out your heart" is not to be taken literally! The reference to people of "low estate" being a "breath" and all of them going "up" in the "balances" is also metaphorical. These are all examples of the way the Scriptures and the life of faith are rich with metaphorical language.

Think, too, of the various metaphors and parables that Jesus used to describe God and the life of faith. In Matthew 13, we are told that the kingdom of heaven is like a mustard seed, yeast, treasure hidden in a field, one pearl of great value, and a net that caught fish of every kind. In John 10, Jesus uses metaphors to explain who he is: "I am the gate" (v. 7) and "I am the good shepherd" (v. 11). Very often these metaphors become so ingrained in our language over time that we no longer recognize them as metaphors. We think of Jesus as literally the "good shepherd," but he was the son of a carpenter, not a shepherd. In the Jesus' time, many of the parables and metaphors were shocking to the hearers, because they were not commonly used, especially in regard to God and, in particular, Jesus' relationship with God. Thus, it is important for us to remind ourselves that, even though the Bible is a written text, the language of faith and our speech about God is and remains metaphorical, a "living language" full of challenging nuance and inspirational surprise.

In fact, even when we speak of characteristics of God such as justice or goodness, we can do so only by analogy. That is, we think of God's justice or goodness in terms of examples of human justice or goodness. Yet God's character is not to be conceived of as somehow quantitatively more of that human quality, but rather, as qualitatively different. God does not simply possess more of the human quality; God's justice or love is by nature different from what we express. It is like the difference between a drawing of a flower and an actual flower. We can know something of God's nature by analogy, but upon reflection, we also realize that God, by nature, differs considerably from human beings and human characteristics. All of this is to say that we need to observe some caution in our language about God and to allow ourselves a certain sense of humility at our inability to name and describe God fully. We need to maintain a sense of awe that we possess any ability to speak of and know the divine in some measure, for it is only by God's gracious self-disclosure that we can begin to describe God.

Many seminaries today have policies related to the use of language in classes and written work. Usually, these policies point to one or two approaches: gender-neutral language and inclusive language. When we use gender-neutral language, we seek to avoid ascribing particular biological characteristics to God. In other words, we do not speak of God as *he* or *him*, *she* or *her*. So rather than saying, "God is good. He is the creator of all things," we would speak in neutral terms: "God is good. God is the creator of all things." Have you noticed that in this book, we have used gender-neutral language for God? Usually, if done with some care, no one even notices the absence of gendered terms. With practice, you will find that referring to God in neutral terms can become second nature. Another preferred gender-neutral term relates to human beings. Rather than speaking of *man* or *mankind* as a term for all people, we use gender-neutral language such as *humanity* or *human beings*.

Inclusive language is similar to gender-neutral language in its intention but tends to suggest a balance in our metaphors for God and people. In some instances, rather than using neutral language, people will say something like "Father God, Mother of us all." Some people find this reference to God as Mother to be shocking. But once we become aware that all language about God is metaphorical, we can see that, in some ways, God is indeed like a mother. In speaking of human beings, inclusive language would offer phrases such as *men and women* or alternate the pronouns: "Sometimes a person is attuned to God. His spirit is open. Her heart is yearning."

When we use inclusive language and gender-neutral language, we aid our pursuit of deliberative theology by carefully reflecting on the fullness of God and the created world. To simply suggest that *man* means "men and women" is a weak argument, demonstrating an embedded theology. If we wish to journey deeper into the reality that is God, we need to stretch beyond the narrow confines of our human pride and routine and honor the power of words to both heal and hurt, reveal and conceal, open and limit our engagement with the divine.

In the book of Exodus, we find a thought-provoking story about Moses and his calling to liberate the people of Israel from the oppression of Egypt. Moses is tending a flock of sheep, minding his own business, when he notices a bush burning but not consumed by the flames, and he turns aside to see it more closely. There he encounters the living God, who announces that Moses is to go to Egypt and free the captives. Moses asks, "Who shall

I tell them sent me?" He wants to know God's name. But the answer is ambiguous: *ehyeh asher ehyeh*, which we translate as "I will be who I will be" or "I am who I am" (3:14). It is a pivotal moment that reminds us we do not have an easy way to name or describe God, since the fullness of God always exceeds our human capacity for expression. We human beings want to get a handle on God, to nail God down, but of course, we tried that once, and God rose again to life—a reality that exceeds our comprehension.

Even framing our use of language as gender neutral or inclusive can "box" God into metaphors that work well only in the context of a particular time, place, and culture. For this reason, I often prefer to speak in terms of "expansive" language. Expansive language suggests that we can never express the fullness of God, but when we expand our vocabulary and images of God, we continue to push against the limits we finite creatures tend to put on who God is. In this way, we do not eliminate the use of father as an image for God or simply balance father with mother, but we constantly seek to find new ways to name God and vary our descriptors. For example, in our prayers we might use any of the following: Gracious God, Merciful God, Alpha and Omega, Holy One, Creator of All, Eternal Love, and so forth. We could even become more poetic, using metaphors

 Define gender-neutral, inclusive, and expansive theological language, and be able to explain why we use these forms of language.

such as O God, Our Fortress; Rock of Our Salvation; or Great Physician of Our Soul. The point is that we should be intentional about varying the ways we name God. I know of one pastor who goes so far as to argue that when we rely exclusively on father language to name God, we are actually lazy and self-centered, falling short of respecting the magnificence and vastness of God. Whether or not you agree with that assessment, our ministry with others will be more effective when we allow ourselves and others to encounter God anew in the varieties of human language.

When I teach students about the shock value of Jesus' own metaphors and how his hearers would have experienced them as strange rather than comforting and common, I sometimes offer my own shocking metaphors to name God. One of my favorites is: "God is a greased pig." You may be quite uncomfortable with this image. Is it respectful and appropriate to say this about God? Of course, God is not literally a greased pig, any more than God is literally a father or a rock. But it does tell us something about how we know God. We human beings chase after God, try to contain God, and just when we think we have gotten our arms firmly around the divine, God slips away again, and we find ourselves face down in the muck, having to renew our attempt to grasp and understand God. Thus, in some ways, God is like a greased pig. Of course, we need to be thoughtful in our use of unusual language. I would not use this particular phrase on Easter or in a funeral sermon. But during ordinary time of the church year, it might wake up and shake up the faithful. Whatever images you choose to speak of God and the life of faith, remember that our theological language will always fall short of the fullness of God. Those are the limits we face as finite creatures. Our task is to recognize and push back against our inclination to control God and make God fit into our small and particular lives, to make God according to our own image and likeness. But the more expansive our language, the less likely we are to fall into the trap of making God into our image, rather than continually and intentionally seeking to know who God is in all God's mystery.

Theological Method: Criteria, Norm, and Sources

Our discussion of theological language leads us now into a survey of theological method. Method, of course, is a process or procedure for doing some task or another, the steps we take, and the tools we use. As we begin to explore theological method, the first point of concern is the criteria we use to evaluate our theology and the norm for this evaluation. While there is no one "correct" theology, since we all see in a mirror dimly, neither do we accept a position of relativism or the idea that anything goes. Being faithful to God requires us to make some judgments with a sense of humility and openness that allows our minds and hearts to be changed over time, rather than simply rejecting proposals that do not match our current set of beliefs. Faithfulness to God is a journey of discovery in which we are carried along within the swirling currents of a river; it is not a steel platform upon which we stand with feet firmly planted and arms crossed, protecting the truth as we know it. Nevertheless, we must always "test the spirits" and seek to discern the adequacy of theological proposals.

Suppose someone creates a theology in which the person holds the words of Benjamin Franklin or a favorite television character as central to his or her understanding of God. Upon what basis might we evaluate such proposals? Would it be *Christian* theology? The criteria we hold—our rules or principles for judgment that form the basis for our evaluation—help us to discern the faithfulness of a theological statement. Keep in mind, of course, that it may not be an all-or-nothing evaluation, in that a theological statement may contain both claims about God and the life of faith that ring true and statements that we might question. Sometimes we refer to this as a hermeneutics of appreciation and critique, in which we interpret the author's statement with an eye toward what is valuable *and* an eye toward what might not speak faithfully about God, therefore inviting us to consider revising or reconstructing it.

Before we consider some criteria that might be useful in evaluating theological proposals, you might have noticed that we are now raising questions about truth claims and the truthfulness of our reflection upon God and the life of faith. These are questions of epistemology, which is the study of knowledge or how we know what we know and how we know what is true. Epistemology is at the heart of Pontius Pilate's question in John 18:38, when he asks, "What is truth?" It is one of the fundamental questions of human beings and one that Christians (and others) have asked of Jesus Christ, the church, and theologians down through the centuries.

This search for what is true also raises questions for us about the authority to make such judgments. Who gets to decide what is true? As we noted in chapter 2, in some traditions, authority is hierarchical. For example, in Roman Catholicism, the judgments of the pope have distinct authority over all other theological statements. For most Protestants, this authority is far more diffuse and democratic, which allows us to discern together the truthfulness of Christian witness but also leads to pronounced disputes among the faithful. Thus, when we refer to "authority," we are pointing to a certain power or sanctioning to decide, to enforce laws or rules, to judge what is acceptable and what is not. Of course, the notion of authority is also contextually situated. For example, a police officer has the authority within her jurisdiction to arrest someone who violates the law, but she does not have that authority in another country. She does not have the authority to enforce the policies of a private company or a denomination. Thus, authority needs to be understood within the particular contexts in which we live and act, and this is also true of the Christian faith.

With the rise of reason during the Enlightenment and the notion of the autonomous individual, the question of authority came under intense scrutiny. Previously, authorities were largely unchallenged, and what a given authority said was essentially the final word. Remember, too, that for generations, the vast majority of people could not read for themselves, even if writings had been widely available, which they were not. But as people became aware of the exercise of reason and as democratic movements began to take hold in France, the United States, and elsewhere, traditional authorities were questioned, and their absolute power was eroded. This questioning of who has the authority to decide continues right down to the present day. Some persons today will go so far as to suggest that the only authority is that of each individual person and his or her understanding. But for Christians who believe that we are not simply autonomous individuals but part of a larger community of faith, the body of Christ, we seek a more moderate position that lies between absolutism in which an external authority decides for us and relativism in which only our own individual preferences matter. Neither extreme is a healthy position for people of faith. If we accept a position of absolutism, then we elevate the institution or another person to God-like status. But if we are unyielding in our own convictions as the only authority by which we live our lives, then we elevate ourselves to God-like status. Instead, we seek a certain give-and-take in the search for truth, and this demands a measure of humility to recognize that sometimes we might be wrong in our judgments or positions and that, together, we can come to a more faithful understanding of our lives in God.

Theological Criteria

We have to be careful, then, not to suggest that any and all Christian witness is faithful witness. We steer a path between our theology or witness being completely and rigidly fixed and it being completely open and unmoored. To do so, we rely on certain criteria to help us assess whether or not a theological proposal is faithful witness. (Even if we do not personally agree with that claim, it may be valid according to the criteria.) There is no one set of criteria that is agreed upon by all theologians, though they tend to point in the same direction. For example, Daniel Migliore defines theology in the classical sense of *fides quaerens intellectum*, or "faith seeking understanding," from which he claims that theology is Christian faith "in the mode of asking questions and struggling to find at least provisional answers to these questions."[1] He then offers four criteria for evaluating theology and the ensuing "proclamation and practice of the community of faith," here paraphrased: (1) Is it true to the revelation of God in Christ in the Scriptures? (2) Is it an adequate expression of the whole revelation in Jesus Christ? (3) Does it represent God as a living reality in the present context? (4) Does it lead to personal and social transformation?[2] We might encapsulate these criteria by indicating that theology should be true, coherent, fitting, and transformative.

Schubert Ogden, by contrast, offers two basic criteria for adjudicating the adequacy of theological proposals: appropriateness and credibility. By "appropriate," Ogden proposes that it "represents the same understanding of faith as is expressed in the . . . normative Christian witness."[3] Ogden thus suggests that theology must be faithful to the stream of witnesses, including Scripture and tradition, that have expressed the Christian faith and been deemed valid by the community of believers. The criterion of credibility means "it meets the relevant conditions of truth universally established with human existence."[4] Is it fitting to our human situation, to our lives in the world today and in each generation? Notice that, unlike Migliore, Ogden is not concerned with transformation, though we might see his criteria as including truth, coherence, and fittingness.

Some liberation theologians, such as James Cone and Elizabeth Johnson, add a specific criterion suggesting theology must be liberating or emancipating to the marginalized and oppressed. This criterion aligns, at least in part, with Migliore's concern for transformation. For liberation theologians, if a theological proposal reinforces unjust structural arrangements that benefit the powerful at the expense of the underprivileged, this criterion would lead them to reject its adequacy in light of the scriptural witnesses.

There are, of course, other ways of configuring and articulating criteria for assessing the validity of theological proposals. It might be helpful for

 Familiarize yourself with the criteria discussed here until you are able to name several of them as a basis for assessing or developing theological proposals.

you to pause and think about what you find most important for assessing any theological position. When you read a theologian or doctrinal statement, on what basis will you assess its authenticity or validity for the life of faith?

Of course, we should also recognize that some denominations have particular criteria for assessing the adequacy of a theological position or Christian practice within that community of faith. The Christian Church,

 Research by Auburn Seminary (www.auburnseminary.org) and others has revealed that many incoming seminarians are not well acquainted with their denomination's theological stance. Check your denomination's website, and compare its statements of faith and practice with those of other church bodies. What are the similarities and the differences?

Disciples of Christ, for example, maintains that believer's baptism is the only valid practice for those churches. United Methodists, in contrast, uphold infant baptism as the preferred practice within their congregations. These are particular theological positions with specific criteria that are central to a tradition's identity and witness to Jesus Christ. In seminary, you will take courses intended to familiarize you with the standards for your denomination, if you belong to one. In my own journey, before I began my seminary studies, I actually read the theological writings that form my denomination's doctrinal standards to make sure that I agreed with those positions and could uphold in my ministry the denomination's criteria for belief and practice. As a result, I found myself more deeply committed to and excited about pursuing ministry within my denomination.

Theological Norm

In some ways, given this sense of finding a middle ground between resisting any change in our theology and being so open that we are largely unmoored, it might feel as if there is no common ground upon which Christian witness can be based. You might wonder if there is some core truth or truths that constitute our Christian faith. Despite the varieties of Christian theology and practice arising from theological reflection, most Christians unite around the norm for doing theology. The norm is the measuring stick or standard by which we can assess the adequacy of our theological proposals and even the adequacy of our criteria. For Christians, we generally point to Jesus Christ, to his life and ministry, his death and resurrection, as the norm for doing theology. In other words, the whole of the biblical witnesses to Jesus. He is, according to Scripture, the way, the truth, and the life (John 14:6). This is our yardstick because in Jesus Christ we have the fullest revelation or self-disclosure of who God is (fully divine) and who we human beings are created to be (fully human). In Jesus Christ, we find the fullest revelation of God but not the final or complete knowledge of God, since it is impossible for the infinite to be fully revealed to the finite.

Of course, our access to Jesus Christ is through the biblical witnesses, and since the gospels provide particular insights into Jesus Christ, we some-

 Make sure that you understand this discussion about the norm and what that means for the practice of theology.

times say that there is a "canon within the canon," in that the gospels hold a privileged position in their witness to Jesus Christ. While we will have more to say about Scripture as a source, Scripture as a whole is sometimes referred to as the *norma normans non normata* (the norm that norms but is not normed). It is akin to saying *sola scriptura*, in that when we want to justify our theological proposals, the revelation in Jesus Christ as attested to in the biblical writings becomes our final measuring stick for adequacy.

Theological Sources

Having established a norm for theology leads us directly into a discussion of the usual sources we draw upon for constructing or assessing theology, as the norm is derived from and supported by these sources and they serve as our tools for faithful reflection. The common sources are Scripture, tradition, reason, and experience, and Scripture is generally deemed to hold the primary place among them for Protestants. Remember that in our historical overview of the development of doctrine, we saw that the earliest theologians drew upon Scripture, and these patristic theologians' writings then became authoritative in the medieval period, thus inaugurating tradition as an important source for theology. The Scholastics then brought reason to the forefront in doing theology. Soon the Reformation emphasis on *sola scriptura* would push back against the privileging of both tradition and reason in doing theology and reemphasize the biblical witnesses (though, in actuality, theology has never been strictly based on Scripture). Finally, in the early modern period, we noted the rise of experience as an important source for theology, though exactly what was meant by experience varied. Today theologians generally engage all four of these sources to one degree or another. We will consider each of these sources in turn, as well as provide a brief introduction to some sources for theology that have been introduced in recent years.

SOURCE: SCRIPTURE

We have already considered the Reformation's emphasis on *sola scriptura*. This principle indicates that Protestants generally view Scripture as the primary source for our Christian theology, doctrine, and practice. Our brief discussion will focus on the notion of inspiration, the authority of Scripture, and principles of hermeneutics (interpretation). The primacy of the Scriptures is often related to the notion of "inspiration" or the idea that the biblical texts have been created under the influence, guidance, or direction of the Holy Spirit. They are in-spired or God-breathed. Most mainline Protestants reject a notion of inspiration that claims it was a supernatural process in which God dictated directly to the biblical scribe, who was merely a mechanical recorder, thus rendering the texts infallible and inerrant. When we read the Scriptures carefully, we notice contradictions and historical realities shaping the texts. Thus, we tend to understand inspiration as the Holy Spirit working in and through human beings who are limited and historically and socially located. At the same time, the Holy Spirit is at work in the readers, proclaimers, interpreters, and hearers down through the centuries, so that the words of Scripture continue to convey spiritual truths or God's word. Thus, when we claim the Scriptures are inspired by God, we affirm that they have a unique character, a relationship to the divine, and contain the guidance and knowledge that is necessary for our salvation. These are sacred texts, and our theology recognizes the central role they play in delineating Christian beliefs and practices.

Although we have already discussed the notion of authority at some length and indicated the difficulties associated with this concept, the authority of Scripture deserves our consideration, given the primacy of the biblical texts to the Christian faith. The early Christian church which arose following the death, resurrection, and ascension of Jesus relied on the authority of its scriptures, which we know today as the Old Testament or the Hebrew Scriptures. Thus, the origins of the church were not a break from the past, but a reinterpretation of it. The early church also viewed the testimony of the apostles who were eyewitnesses to Jesus as authoritative to this new way of being God's people, but primarily because this testimony pointed directly to the authority of Jesus as the Messiah, as the one they proclaimed as Lord and as the Word incarnate. He himself was and is the reinterpretation of and continuity with God's salvation history. When the canon of Scripture was formed—and the testimony of the eyewitnesses became part of the New Testament writings—these authorities were communally affirmed. Later Christian writings were also affirmed as authentic witnesses to the way of Jesus Christ, even if their authors had not been present with Jesus in the flesh. At the same time, we should recognize that Christians have also believed in the authority of Scripture as a result of the Holy Spirit testifying to the faithful about the sacred nature of this word. Thus, it is not only because the human community affirms this authority, but because God acts to attest to it in the lives of believers.

Daniel Migliore's discussion of inadequate approaches to the question of biblical authority is helpful in guiding our understanding.[5] Notice here that sometimes our theological inquiry is aided by attending to what something is not. (In relation to our understanding of God, we would call this method of inquiry the *via negativa*.) Migliore argues, first, against the "bib-

---

 The term *plenary* is derived from the Latin word *plenus*, meaning full or complete. In some theological circles, it has come to mean absolute and unchangeable.

---

licist view" of plenary inspiration, in which the authority is located strictly in the supernatural character of the words, which are thought to correspond exactly to God's words. Again, this points to the idea of the human writer as little more than a scribe in the hands of the Holy Spirit. But this viewpoint tends to elevate the words of the Scriptures into a position of ultimacy, rather than holding the Word or the living and active God as the ultimate and final authority. Even the Bible can become an idol or idolatrous if we place it above God or treat it as if it were God. This view of authority also neglects to recognize the cultured and contextual elements of the Scriptures in different historical eras and settings, and it ignores some texts while fiercely upholding and privileging others that better support an interpreter's theological positions.

The second error in approaches to biblical authority is one that arose in the modern era: the view that the Bible is a historical document. As a historical document, the Bible is treated as an artifact in which the task of reconstructing the facts—the history, linguistics, culture, and archaeological evidence—of the texts is of primary importance. Of course, the historical-critical method has been an important tool in deepening our understanding of biblical texts and aiding our interpretation, but when the texts are viewed as simply a historical relic, their broader meaning and the sweep of the biblical narrative have been lost. We might say that the historical realities of the Scriptures are insightful and contribute significantly to our understanding but do not comprise the fullness of the scriptural message of salvation by faith.

A third error is similar in nature, as it treats the Bible as ancient literature, worthy of study in a literature course. The error here, no doubt, is that for communities of faith, these are not just stories about characters, but living witnesses to the reality of God, Jesus Christ, and the Holy Spirit at work in the world, and this reality has transformative power in the lives of people today.

Finally, Migliore touches on a tendency that arises in modernity, which is the attempt to view scriptural authority as an individualistic and private matter associated with personal devotion. While personal devotion is a part of our lives in God, the Christian faith is, by its very nature, communal, and the biblical witnesses testify to the corporate nature of our faith. To be in Christ is to be incorporated into the community of believers. The Word comes alive where two or three are gathered, and it sends Christians into the world as bearers of this witness. Of course, at times we all read (or should read) the Bible devotionally, as guidance and encouragement for our own lives. But the Scriptures are not intended to be simply a private and personal source of inspiration, and their authenticity lies in the communal accountability from generation to generation.

Migliore's identification of missteps in locating the nature of scriptural authority helps us focus on how to delineate the contours of that authority for our lives as Christians in the twenty-first century. This authority is found in the communal nature of the Scriptures in the full sweep of the witnesses to God's salvation history that culminates in Jesus of Nazareth, who is the Christ. Because Jesus Christ is the norm and the Scriptures are *norma normans non normata*, they authorize our theological proposals, what we believe and how we practice our faith. No one text of the Bible provides singular authority, but rather each passage in the context of the whole message of salvation history—how God is at work for our redemption and reconciliation in and through Jesus Christ; therein lies the authority for our theological proposals.

Of course, even as we recognize this authoritative status, the very nature of Scripture leads us to the concern for hermeneutics, or the interpretation of Scripture. The interpretation of Scripture is a fact of our human existence and finitude, though some people argue that the Bible can and should be read literally. Imagine, for a moment, that you are living in the Middle Ages. You know nothing of the Enlightenment or the modern mind-set. Electronics and wireless communications do not exist; in fact, there isn't electricity and running water. There are no public libraries or bookstores, no newspapers we pick up on the street corner. We don't each have a Bible or two or three lying around the house. We believe that the earth is the center of the universe. It's hard to imagine what life would be like in the twelfth century, and harder still to grasp how human beings viewed and understood their lives and world. There can be little doubt that the people of each generation necessarily understand the biblical witnesses in the light of their own horizon, in the midst of their own social and intellectual milieu.

Yet the Bible has been and remains central to the way we understand and live our Christian lives in the world and in each distinctive era of human history. Alister McGrath goes so far as to suggest that "the history of Christian theology can be regarded as the history of biblical interpretation."[6] The timelessness of the Word of God is always spoken and heard anew in each generation. We know that we bring a certain lens to our reading and understanding of the biblical texts. In fact, we might claim that the Word became flesh and dwelt among us as a model and reminder that the Word becomes incarnate in each generation and, more so, in each cultural expression of human life. The Word remains relevant and meaningful, not trapped in the human history and cultures of the past. Thus, interpretation should be viewed not as something negative or unfortunate, but rather, as an expression of how God meets us in the particulars of the world across time and space. We will have more to say about the importance of context later in this chapter, but for now, our goal is to recognize that Scripture is necessarily interpreted whenever we human beings read it. There is no human being who reads devoid of certain frames of reference and presuppositions. There was no biblical author who was free of such frames of reference and presuppositions.

Remember, too, that we previously considered how theologians from the earliest days of the church, such as Origen and Augustine, began to articulate different levels of meaning at work in the Scriptures. This practice of discerning the various meanings continued to shape the use of the Bible as a source for theology throughout Christian history and suggests that approaches to interpretation have long been associated with Scripture as a source for our Christian beliefs and practice. In the medieval era, Thomas Aquinas articulated four levels ("senses") of meaning in the Scriptures: the literal plus a threefold spiritual sense of allegorical (the Old Testament allegorically referencing the New Testament and in cases where the literal meaning is cloudy), moral or tropological (how Christians should act), and anagogical (referencing the hope beyond this world). Not all passages would necessarily contain all senses of Scripture, but these different meanings were deemed to be at work within the Bible. To excavate any meaning is to enter into interpretation.

Elisabeth Schüssler Fiorenza, a feminist scholar of biblical interpretation and theology, provides us with a contemporary example of the ongoing work of interpreting Scripture. She offers a critical feminist biblical interpretation aimed at liberation, which consists of four "key moments": (1) a hermeneutics of suspicion (scrutinizing presuppositions); (2) historical remembrance and reconstruction (sociopolitical and historical analysis);

 Compare patristic interpretative levels on page 18 with Schüssler Fiorenza's interpretive method summarized here.

(3) proclamation or ethical and theological evaluation (assessing liberatory and oppressive trajectories); and (4) creative imagination and ritualization (retelling and reliving).[7] For Schüssler Fiorenza, this "model of feminist

biblical interpretation . . . challenges other modes of biblical reading to become more comprehensive and sophisticated."[8] Ultimately, this interpretative process is aimed at the transformation of both church and society for the sake of the flourishing of all persons. While this view of hermeneutics may stretch your understanding and even unsettle you a bit, each new generation of interpreters has challenged, stretched, and unsettled the last one across the centuries. Interpretation is a never-ending reality when we engage the scriptural witnesses.

But if interpretation is always occurring and if we all have particular lenses we bring to our reading of the Bible, how do we avoid misleading or unfaithful interpretations of Scripture? The first thing to be said is that unfaithful interpretations abound. In his Second Letter to the Corinthians, Paul railed against the interpreters, "super-apostles," whose message was inconsistent with the teachings of Jesus (11:4-5). In our own day, countless examples of the "prosperity gospel" can be found in churches large and small teaching that a person's belief in God will lead him or her to be healthy, wealthy, and wise (which, of course, is the gospel according to Benjamin Franklin, not Jesus Christ). Clearly, we need some principles to enable the truthfulness and faithfulness of our interpretations of Scripture, including what is proclaimed from the pulpit and taught in the Sunday school.

The principles or guidance for evaluating interpretations may vary but tend to include several basic considerations. First, given the theological norm derived from the life and teachings of Jesus Christ, interpretations of Scripture should be consistent with the overall message of salvation history and the mission of God in the world. In other words, there is an overarching sense conveyed by Scripture, and any interpretation should be consistent with that message, particularly in the witnesses to Jesus Christ. If we interpret a particular verse or text apart from the broader meaning of the Scriptures, our interpretation might well be off track. If we resort to "proof-texting" (choosing individual texts to support our position), we may be taking those passages out of context to suit our own purposes.

Second, we should take seriously the historical-critical method of biblical study by which we examine the context of the time, place, and circumstances in which the biblical author wrote. By doing so, we can begin to discern the human elements that are inevitably present in any text, as well as to highlight the movement of God in history so that our focus is on

God's salvific work. Studying the original context of a text enables us to interpret it responsibly within our own horizon, in terms that make sense today but are faithful to the witness of the past. For example, while we no longer use a denarius as form of payment, by examining the original context we can suggest what a denarius might be worth today. But will we make that comparison based upon a typical day's wages or upon its worth in the price of silver today? Should we assume a typical laborer's wages in the contemporary United States' context would approximate those in the ancient world? As you can see, even the historical-critical method requires us to make hermeneutical moves.

Third, because the Bible is the church's book, a communal document, interpretations should be accountable to the larger community of faith. Of course, seldom will an interpretation be deemed valid by all Christians, since we also interpret through our own lenses, even though some will claim to be unbiased readers. But keep in mind that the way an African villager reads a text may draw on metaphors largely incomprehensible to Christians in Stockholm. A farmer in rural Nebraska may relate well to Jesus' agricultural metaphors and expand upon the notion of a mustard seed or one lost sheep among a flock. But in the middle of New York City or Buenos Aires, the agricultural metaphors may not be the most appropriate and relevant way to convey the message of the gospel. Thus, different communities of faith will inevitably allow the scriptural interpretation to translate into the lives of the hearers in all their particularity. Yet this does not affirm every individual interpretation as valid; it continues to depend upon the discernment of the larger community of faith.

The significance of scripture for Protestants, its inspiration, authority, and interpretative nature all point toward the basic theological concept of Scripture as the Word of God. Not all the words of Scripture should be equated directly with the Word of God, which we might consider a manifestation of the nature and will of God, the revelation of the divine reality. Karl Barth's expression of the threefold Word of God is helpful in directing us toward this unique character of Scripture, though it is not the only way to convey the scope of God's Word. For Barth, the Word is first and foremost the Word become flesh, Jesus Christ. It is secondly the Word become flesh in the form of Scripture. Third, the Word of God is present and revealed in the proclamation of the church. In all three forms, God is manifest in our lives. Thus, when we use Scripture as a source for theology it is not the words of the Scripture that carry the weight, but the Word as God's presence, revelation, and guidance for our life together as people of faith.

SOURCE: TRADITION

The second source for doing theology is tradition, a word that comes from the Latin *tradere*, meaning "to hand down." For Christians, it represents the "handing down" of the beliefs and practices that the church holds to be authoritative and faithful to the life and teachings of Jesus Christ. Another

 Define tradition, but be sure to make note of the ambiguity surrounding this term.

way of describing tradition is to say that those things Christians have held dear and claimed to be true continue to serve as companions for the faith journey in subsequent generations. These beliefs and practices help to shape our identity as Christians. But by now, you should be attuned to the streams of Christian theology that have emerged over the centuries and might well ask: Which identity? Which church? Which community or communities of Christians is the "tradition?" The answer, as you might expect, depends upon where you stand, which is not necessarily a bad thing.

As we have seen, tradition emerged as a source initially in the medieval era, when Christian theologians reiterated and even organized the teachings of the patristic writers. But the tension between privileging tradition or Scripture came to the forefront during the Reformation, as the Reformers questioned the validity of some of the teachings and practices of the Catholic tradition. Moreover, the Reformation marks a distinct branching off of the tradition from Roman Catholicism (of course, Catholics do not officially accept the validity of the Protestant churches as part of the true church). In other words, tradition is not a single, static deposit of teachings that all Christians hold in common. In Protestant churches, the stream of the tradition leading up to the Reformation is not rejected but finds voice and expression in the theology of Luther, Calvin, Wesley, and others.

Think of your own denomination and its tradition. What are the teachings and practices that are handed down from generation to generation? For a Presbyterian, Calvin's *Institutes* would be considered part of the tradition, but not for Methodists, who would hand down the writings of John Wesley. In the African Methodist Episcopal Church, John Wesley's theology forms part of the tradition, but its founder, Richard Allen, would represent a distinct divergence from the early Methodist tradition in America. For the Christian Church, Disciples of Christ, the tradition would include the Stone-Campbell Movement, but not so for American Baptists, who would include Roger Williams and John Clarke. If you are unsure of the tradition as embraced by your own church or denomination, it will be helpful to search online or ask a pastor to point you toward the fundamental documents and voices that shape the tradition to which you belong. Remember that theology is a stream, and we step into that stream at a particular point; gazing back from that point, we can see the tradition that has preceded us. Our Christian identity is shaped by the tradition in which we are located. We may follow the one Christ, but we express our lives in Christ in a variety of ways that continue to be handed down from generation to generation.

SOURCE: REASON

As theology evolved, the Scholastic theologians first brought reason to the forefront, and then the modern era elevated reason as the highest of human capacities. Kant's book *Religion within the Limits of Reason Alone* is representative of the turn to reason that characterized the modern mind-set. There was an emerging sense that the rational mind, the capacity to think, was a sufficient basis for discovering knowledge for everything, including God, apart from revelation. The modern emphasis on rationalism—the sense of the sufficiency of reason alone—should be distinguished from the human capacity to reason, which exists apart from arguments related to its purposes and ultimate goal. The exercise of reason as a source for theology has been both a positive force and, in the extreme as rationalism, an impediment or complication to the pursuit of theology.

When we consider that unquestioned and unchecked authority has often led to the oppression of others and unequal societies, the rise of reason marked an important shift in human understanding. Where once church and civil authorities could make decisions unilaterally, the rise of reason opened up a certain accountability to the masses and, more importantly, accountability to God. Just because a church leader or priest says something is of God doesn't mean it is necessarily the case. And the ability to reason and ask questions has proven over time to further the reign of God on earth as we critique and affirm teachings. In retrospect, we can reflect upon past Christian practices such as the Crusades or the support of many churches for slavery and recognize that these things were not God's will. Reason can be life giving in this sense.

It is also clear that we have been given the gift of intellect to ponder the meaning of life and our faith. There is no thought we might think that is not known already to God; we need not fear asking questions about God and the life of faith. Indeed, in the gospels, we find Jesus using logic and reason. For example, when he is asked about the paying of taxes, he responds, " 'Show me a denarius. Whose head and whose title does it bear?' They said, 'The emperor's.' He said to them, 'Then give to the emperor the things that are the emperor's, and to God the things that are God's' " (Luke 20:24-25). You have heard the phrase, "Jesus is the reason." But, perhaps, we should revise it to say that "Jesus used his reason." This gift from God should be widely embraced by the faithful.

But, of course, there are also limits to reason. While the modern perspective elevated reason to the primary—indeed, at times sole—source of reliable knowledge and suggested its exercise could lead to the good society and human excellence, our experience over time has proven the sheer fallacy of that supposition. Weaponry has become increasingly more destructive. Drugs that target a disease create side effects that are equally debilitating. We cannot think our way to the perfect society. We cannot think our way to God, despite the claims of rationalists. The modernist argument, from Ludwig Feuerbach, Sigmund Freud, and others, that God is merely a human projection of deep-seated desires, wishes, or fears has not been proven true or widely accepted. Human beings continue to hold a widespread belief in God, even if they are increasingly rejecting or disavowing organized religion.

Theologians have long argued that, as a result of the fall from grace, our reason is corrupted, which means that, unaided by grace, we do not have clear and correct knowledge, especially of God. Yet even as Christians believe there is a limit to the exercise of reason, it does not mean we deny scientific evidence. We need not place faith in opposition to reason or science or fact. The theory of evolution or advances in genetics are not incompatible with Christian faith, as we believe that God has placed in motion physical laws and created an orderly, reliable universe. We experience our physical environment as orderly and reliable, so much so that we seldom reflect upon it. We do not awaken each morning wondering if there will be a sun or a sky. A surgeon does not have to wonder where in the body she will find the heart or liver. We know what a dog is or a cat because their characteristics remain remarkably stable even as breeds vary. We live in an orderly and organized universe.

Most theologians consider scientific evidence as an aid to deepen our theological understanding, whereas denying the knowledge obtained through science leads to theological proposals that lack credibility in our contemporary society. Suppose we were to suggest, as Bishop Ussher did in the seventeenth century, that creation occurred in the year 4004 BCE. Today we have scientific evidence obtained through radiometric dating of rocks and other archaeological techniques that falsify Ussher's chronology. How likely are nonbelievers to take seriously a theological claim that is disproven by scientific evidence? Were we to insist on Ussher's dating of the earth, we would appear silly to most nonbelievers, so much so they would be closed to the possibility of faith. Of course, there are some Christians today who still hold to that claim of creation in 4004 BCE, but without the exercise of reason—and the recognition that reason is a capacity given to us by God—Christian theology and faith lack credibility and intelligibility. Thus, theology utilizes logic, reason, and evidence to formulate proposals that are meaningful and true, but reason inevitably remains one tool among others, and it does not resolve all the mysteries of human existence or provide answers to the nature and will of God. As McGrath puts it, "A central theme of Christian theology down the ages has been that the human attempts to discern fully the nature and purposes of God are ultimately unsuccessful."[9] While McGrath chooses to emphasize God's sovereignty and transcendence, we also do come to know important dimensions of the nature and purposes of God that inform our life in the world. Christians understand there is a limit to our knowledge, particularly when God is the subject of our inquiry, but we also live and live abundantly according to that which can be known.

Because reason as a source for theology has its limits, Christians have traditionally embraced the meaning and function of revelation in theology. Revelation, by definition, refers to the disclosure of something previously hidden, stemming from the Greek word *apokalypto*, which means to uncover or disclose. George Stroup helpfully distinguishes revelation's "objective" dimension, "*what* is revealed," from its "subjective" dimension,

Define revelation and how it functions in relation to theology. Make sure you are clear on the distinction between the objective and subjective dimensions of revelation.

or "*how* revelation is received."[10] In traditional theology up through the seventeenth century, the objective side generally referred to either the Word of God as revealed in Jesus Christ or a particular teaching of Scripture or the church. The subjective side was considered "some form of illumination. God illumines the mind so that it can see what it cannot see by means of reason alone."[11] Revelation requires both the objective (the what) and the subjective (the how) working together.

One further clarification about revelation should be offered, related to what we are calling the subjective side of revelation, or how we receive this knowledge of God. Often we distinguish between general revelation, in which God is disclosed in nature and in the conscience of people and thus is available to all, and special revelation, whereby God is revealed in specific events in salvation history and above all in the incarnation of Jesus. Special revelation is accessed by means of faith. In the case of Christian faith, revelation is God's self-disclosure to humanity in the form of Jesus Christ and through the events of salvation history recorded in the biblical texts, though admittedly the human reception of revelation is not without its difficulties. We might say that the revelation of God is filtered through our limited and sinful human lives, through our corrupt reason, which is why we are urged to take on "the mind of Christ" (1 Cor. 2:16). Christianity thus claims its origin lies in God's revelation, God's free act of self-disclosure, rather than through human construction. In other words, our reason is able to take us only so far, and revelation provides us with knowledge that would otherwise remain unavailable to human beings.

But with the Enlightenment's turn to reason and the growing critique of civil and church authorities, traditional notions of revelation were challenged, and this process shaped our understanding in the twentieth century. Various responses were proposed to respond intelligibly to such challenges, including the emphasis on moral and ethical grounds for Christian faith apart from the reliance on God found in classic liberalism. Karl Barth's neo-orthodoxy responded with a reemphasis on the absolute necessity of revelation with his concept of the threefold Word of God. In many ways, versions of both of these modern expressions of revelation—that of classic liberalism and the response of neo-orthodoxy—continue to inform Christian theology. Stroup concludes that contemporary theology wrestles with four issues in understanding revelation: (1) what we mean when we speak of God's agency in an event of disclosure, (2) how interpretation functions in our reception of revelation, (3) how we authenticate true interpretations of revelatory events, and (4) how Christian revelation relates to other religions.[12] Christians, for the most part, continue to believe that much of our knowledge of God and the life of faith can be accessed only by means of God's revelation, but God's self-disclosure is neither straightforward nor uncomplicated, if we thoughtfully seek to understand God and human existence.

SOURCE: EXPERIENCE

The last common source or tool for theological reflection is experience. Here again, we find that engaging experience as a source for theology is somewhat complicated. Remember that experience came to the forefront during the modern era. In the eighteenth century, John Wesley critiqued the growing rationalism and deism of his day and argued that the Church of England had the form of religion without the substance or power of God. We might say he perceived his church as going through the motions. The theology and practice of his Methodist movement, a renewal movement that would grow to become numerous denominations, added experience to the Anglican triad of Scripture, tradition, and reason. Wesley's use of the term *experience* referred primarily, though not exclusively, to the experience of God in the life of believers. This often took the form of the assurance of one's faith or a personal experience of the saving grace of God, which represents classic eighteenth-century "evangelicalism." For Wesley, this experience of God, while individual, was inevitably accountable to the community of faith, as he claimed there is no personal holiness without social holiness, and vice versa. Thus, this experience or assurance of God's salvific work, as confirmed by the community of faith, is an important source for theological reflection.

In the nineteenth century, a second expression of experience as a theological source was articulated by Friedrich Schleiermacher. The phrase that best expresses Schleiermacher's understanding is "a feeling of absolute dependence," found in his major work, *The Christian Faith*. Schleiermacher rejects the notion that Christian faith is based in intellectual assent, and instead suggests that this feeling of our utter and complete dependence

 Consider the different ways of speaking about "experience" and how theologians have defined this important source.

on the infinite, something beyond human capacities, forms the basis for understanding the Christian faith: "*the consciousness of being absolutely dependent, or, which is the same thing, of being in relation with God.*"[13] This religious experience to which Schleiermacher points is an awareness of God and our human finitude; it is a particular kind of experience and not merely any event or emotion we might encounter. Much like Wesley's treatment of the subject in the eighteenth century, Schleiermacher's emphasis on experience has a particular content that is dependent upon God's presence in the life of the believer.

In contemporary theological expressions, experience continues to be an important source, though two clear distortions are particularly present. The first is a theological distortion, and the second is an individualistic one. In the theological distortion of experience as a source for theological reflection, we find some churches teaching that the essence of Christian faith is simply a personal relationship with Jesus Christ, such that Jesus becomes "my" personal savior, and experience is reduced to my emotional connection to Jesus. Although theologians such as Wesley and Schleiermacher have illuminated the importance of the experience of God, this experience was never conceived as the fullness of the Christian faith, but rather an impetus toward living in relationship to God and others. Of course, there is a place for teaching about the experience of and relationship with Jesus Christ. Our point here is that when that personal experience becomes equated with the fullness of the faith, personal experience has been elevated to a privileged position that leads believers to neglect important dimensions of the Christian life attested to by the Scriptures. The tendency toward individualism and autonomy characteristic of the modern era finds expression in this personalization of Jesus, almost as a sort of a personal possession.

The individualistic distortion occurs when experience is more broadly conceived as any experience or feeling encountered by an individual apart from any communal accountability. In this case, someone resorts to his or her own experience as the sole authority for beliefs and practices. For example, suppose someone claims to be a Christian but holds to the belief and practice that God calls him to spend Sundays walking in the woods or sitting by a lake. His experience tells him that in these natural settings, he feels closest to God, so the church is not where he should practice his faith. Thus, his experience apart from Scripture, tradition, and reason is guiding his understanding of the Christian life. In some ways, we might view this tendency as both a product of modernity's emphasis on the individual and a rejection of its privileging of reason and rationality.

But let's consider this example through the theological lenses of Scripture, tradition, and reason to discern whether or not spending each Sunday alone in nature seems to be a faithful and true theological position. If we turn first to Scripture, what evidence might we bring to bear on this question? Certainly, in the negative sense, we do not find passages where Jesus or Paul or other biblical witnesses present this option as a valid one. But an argument from absence of evidence may not be our strongest case. Instead, we could consider passages that demonstrate the communal nature of faith found throughout the Hebrew Scriptures and New Testament. Certainly, the biblical witnesses regularly recount how those communities go astray and must be called back to authentic life in God. To some, that might seem a good basis for rejecting the community as necessary to the life of faith, but if we are unable to discern the will of God clearly together, what evidence do we have that one individual can be more faithful in discernment than a community? And while it is true that Jesus took time apart from the community, he inevitably did so only in order to return to the disciples and the people renewed in spirit and purpose. Thus, if someone is walking in the woods rather than worshipping with the community, if it is for the purpose of returning with a deeper commitment to the common life, then we might consider that to be a valid expression. Here you might want to pause and consider other scriptural texts that could help you to assess the validity of walking in nature as a Christian practice in lieu of worship.

The second source for considering this question is the teachings of the tradition or, better, the traditions that compose the Christian faith. Where might we turn for insights into whether a person's decision to "worship" alone in nature might be considered a valid Christian belief and practice? We might want to begin with what our specific denomination has to say about the church and the life of worship. Or perhaps return to the patristic writings to gain a clearer sense of the origins of Christian worship and what it meant to worship God on a regular basis as a community. Augustine, for example, drew a sharp distinction between nature and grace, claiming that our life in God depends upon the presence of grace. Cyprian first claimed, "There is no salvation outside the church," and we might wish to explore his rationale for that claim. So we might ask whether there are particular practices by which we receive God's grace. Here, we might reflect upon the sacraments that incorporate us into the church and offer ongoing reconciliation and whether nature is able to substitute for the sacraments as understood by the long stream of Christians. Again, you might have other questions or considerations in relation to the tradition that could help you to wrestle with the question.

Finally, when we come to the exercise of reason—which we have already been engaging in our consideration of Scripture and tradition—we might find a host of questions and logical concerns. Is faith a private and individual matter, or is there an inescapably communal dimension? What are the marks of discipleship, and can they be seen in a person whose faith is primarily about a solitary relationship to God? What is missing in this form of worship and discipleship? Can the person rightly consider himself to be a Christian? What is the basis for making such a claim? Who has the authority to decide? Ultimately, can this person do as he pleases with no consequences? And if there are consequences, are they earthly, otherworldly, or something else entirely? You can probably add to this list, and I would encourage you to spend a few moments thinking about other questions you might ask through the exercise of reason.

As we can see from this short reflective exercise, careful and deliberate theological reflection depends upon more than one source, and claiming personal experience as the one valid authority for our faith is fraught with pitfalls and blind spots. It may be the case that, in the contemporary era, many people depend upon personal experience as the sole basis for evaluating their lives and their Christian faith. When this occurs, there is no scriptural, historical, or reasoned basis by which to change our mind. Thus, we become our own arbiter of truth, simply because we feel a particular way. But theological reflection on God and the content of the Christian faith inevitably requires us to be open to a journey of discovery. Faith in God is not a static condition, but involves an ongoing process of seeking to know and understand God more fully. In the final estimation, experience remains an important source for doing theology, but it must be placed into conversation with other sources and within the accountability of a community of faith.

MORE RECENT SOURCES

Before we conclude our discussion of sources, we should note the introduction and use of other sources for theological reflection in recent decades. In Black Theology, for example, theologians have drawn on slave narratives and the blues or spirituals as authentic expressions of Christian faith. Contemporary Native American theologians incorporate traditional Native ways into their theological projects, recognizing that God had been present to them before Christian faith arrived on the continent. While some people might take exception to these newer sources, we should also remember that each of the sources we have discussed—Scripture, tradition, reason, and experience—was developed in response to the realities of a given theological era. Thus, the stream of theology will likely continue to encounter new ways of engaging and developing faithful witness to God.

CULTURE AND CONTEXT

These newer sources for doing theology, in many cases, arise out of and in response to particular cultural contexts. For generations, theology was the exclusive domain of educated men, often propertied and frequently white or European. The theological statements they produced were considered to be universally applicable or appropriate for every human being. Their theologies were posited as "neutral" or being largely free of context. But as theologians of color and women began to publish theologies beginning in the 1970s, taking into account their social and cultural locations and claiming such locations as essential to their authentic Christian witness, these newer voices often faced criticism for naming their context and culture. Identified as "contextual theologies," the theologies that take seriously cultural and social locations, often those of minoritized racial and ethnic groups, were often marginalized by the majority culture, which claims such contextual theologies are relevant only to a particular culture or group, thereby having limited value. As diverse voices continued to enter and shape the theological

Consider the meaning of culture and how it shapes our lives as well as beliefs and practices.

landscape, they could not be ignored and, in recent years, have begun to shift our understanding of the influence of context for doing theology. However, we should be clear that there are theologians today who continue to marginalize or ignore the theologies that engage cultural contexts.

Culture can be defined as a way of life or of organizing communities according to particular values, morals, practices, and social norms that are transmitted from generation to generation through language and material forms. We all live within multiple cultures such as those of our family, church, nation, region, racial or ethnic group, and so forth. But some cultural contexts take on greater significance in shaping our lives and understanding of the world. While some theologians continue to hold the view that Christian faith is context-free and should be universal, we also know that God became flesh in Jesus of Nazareth within a particular context at a particular time. God's action in the incarnation seems to affirm the particularity of our human existence rather than to deny its importance. So we have a certain scriptural basis for contextualizing and claiming the embodiment of our theologies.

How, then, has this sense of culture and context reshaped theological method in recent decades? First, we have come to realize that no theology is neutral or context-free. The majority culture in any society considers its perspective and cultural characteristics as normative, which means those who belong to that dominant culture might seldom encounter and experience other cultural standards and expressions. But no culture is neutral; they are all value-laden. Churches often claim to be open to persons of different cultures, races, and ethnicities, but what they really mean is they are open to diverse persons so long as any new members adhere to existing cultural norms. Often white Americans do not see themselves as having a race or a particular culture because they compose the majority culture. When we consider that the membership of the mainline churches in the United States hovers around 90 percent white non-Hispanic, even though the U.S. population as a whole is only around 64 percent white non-Hispanic, we begin to see that, to minoritized groups, the majority culture's context perhaps does not feel welcoming and open. Such is the case with theology as well. All theologies are products of particular contexts and cultures, despite claims to be neutral.

Second, in the modern era, the height of theological production was the creation of a systematic theology that examined the whole of the Christian faith, doctrine by doctrine. In recent theology, however, fewer comprehensive theological systems have been written, due at least in part to the growing sense that no one person can create a theology that is fitting, relevant, and meaningful for all contexts. Thus, contemporary theology textbooks are often written by a group of scholars from different perspectives, rather than one author. Theologies are written from a wide variety of perspectives by persons from across the globe. On the surface, this proliferation of voices may appear to be a fragmentation of the discipline or even the Christian faith, but the future is likely to witness even more diversity, given the widespread use of technology including social media, blogs, and so on. Of course, there has never been a time when a single theologian could speak for all people, in the best interest of all people, and in terms that were meaningful to all. Knowing that human beings are finite creatures incapable of the infinite, we can conclude that no single person has the capacity to express the fullness of the faith in a timeless and universal fashion. The cacophony of voices on today's theological landscape offers a wealth of insights into the reality of God and the life of faith, and you will have to learn to navigate these vastly different projects.

Later in this book, I will ask you to write your first "credo," or statement of what you believe. In preparation for writing your credo, you might want to spend some time considering how your context or contexts and the different cultures you inhabit shape the way you understand and live out your Christian faith. What might you learn about God by encountering theologies that arise out of other contexts with which you are not familiar?

Orienting Concerns or Starting Points for Theology

The last area for our consideration in this brief overview of theological method is the central concern or starting point for doing theology, which shapes our theological method. The theological movements of the twentieth century can help us see these methodological concerns more concretely. Though my synopsis here risks oversimplification, its point is to suggest that theologies can often be identified and unpacked when we are able to identify a central orienting concern or overarching theme that drives or defines the theologian's project. It is a question we can ask of any theology so we can better understand or discern the method at work.

Karl Barth's neo-orthodox theology, for example, is centered in the premise of the Wholly Other God, or God's utter transcendence and inaccessibility to human beings apart from the revelation of God in the threefold Word of Jesus Christ, the Scriptures, and the church's proclamation. The sovereignty and transcendence of God undergirds or weaves together his theology. Conversely, Paul Tillich's theology begins with the human being and the existential concern or anxiety over the possibility of nonbeing, of estrangement, and of ambiguity and fragmentation. His method thus correlates these philosophical questions with the answers provided by the Christian message: Being-Itself (God), Jesus the Christ as the New Being, and the Spirit. When we recognize that his theology is driven by this central concern for the angst of the human being in existential doubt, we begin to see it at work throughout his writings. For liberation theologians such as James Cone and Ada María Isasi-Díaz, the starting point or pivot point is the liberation of the oppressed, sometimes framed as a "preferential option for the poor" or marginalized and powerless. It is this reference to the lived experience of the people in the face of systemic injustices that leads into theological reflection as a second moment of engaging God. Finally, in relational theologies, we note that the interrelationship of all life, even the cosmos, is the orienting concern for these theological projects. This basic premise of interrelationship will guide and shape the theological project and serve as a key basis for its coherence.

Thus, when we read a theological work, if we are able to identify this starting point or central concern, our comprehension will be aided considerably. If we begin to write our own credo, reflecting first on our own central theological concern and our starting point in the transcendence of God, the existential situation of the human being, God's desire for liberation and the flourishing of life, or the relationality of God's created order will enable us to address our own deepest-held beliefs with care and coherence. Of course, while identifying a starting point or central concern enables us to uncover and articulate the theological method present in a theology, it remains a preliminary step in the real task of doing theology: delineating the content of the Christian faith, the doctrines or teachings that shape our Christian identity. Chapter 4 will take us on that journey into the heart of theology, our basic beliefs.

Questions for Personal Exploration

1. What do we mean by "gender-neutral," "inclusive," and "expansive" theological language? Why is our use of language so central to theology?
2. How would you describe what a theological method is and does? How do the norm and criteria relate to a theological method? How would you begin to describe your own theological method for articulating what you believe?
3. Return to the discussion of whether walking alone in the woods every week is a faithful substitute for Christian worship. How does each of the sources for theology help us reflect upon this question? Which source carries the most weight for your deliberations, and why?
4. If you were to name your central concern in writing about what you believe as a Christian, what would it be and why?

Resources for Deeper Exploration

Any good systematic theology textbook will cover the topics associated with theological method. See, for example, David Tracy, "Theological Method," and Edward Farley and Peter C. Hodgson, "Scripture and Tradition," in *Christian Theology: An Introduction to Its Traditions and Tasks*, rev. ed., ed. Peter C. Hodgson and Robert H. King (Minneapolis: Fortress Press, 1994), 35–60 and 61–87.

Allen, Paul L. *Theological Method: A Guide for the Perplexed.* Guides for the Perplexed. London: T&T Clark, 2012.

Bohler, Caroline Jane. *God the What? What Our Metaphors for God Reveal about Our Beliefs in God.* Woodstock, VT: Skylight Paths, 2008.

Jasper, David. *A Short Introduction to Hermeneutics.* Louisville: Westminster John Knox, 2004.

Kaufman, Gordon. *An Essay on Theological Method.* 3rd ed. Atlanta: Scholars, 1995.

Schüssler Fiorenza, Elisabeth. "The Bible, the Global Context, and the Discipleship of Equals." In *Reconstructing Christian Theology*, edited by Rebecca S. Chopp and Mark Lewis Taylor. Minneapolis: Fortress Press, 1994.

Tanner, Kathryn. *Theories of Culture: A New Agenda for Theology.* Minneapolis: Fortress Press, 1997.

👀 Notes

1. Daniel L. Migliore, *Faith Seeking Understanding*, 2nd ed. (Grand Rapids: Eerdmans, 2004), 3.

2. Ibid., 11–15.

3. Schubert Ogden, "What Is Theology?" in *On Theology* (San Francisco: Harper & Row, 1986), 4.

4. Ibid., 5.

5. Migliore, *Faith Seeking Understanding*, 47–50.

6. Alister E. McGrath, *Christian Theology: An Introduction*, 4th ed. (Malden, MA: Blackwell, 2007), 129.

7. Elisabeth Schüssler Fiorenza, "The Bible, the Global Context, and the Discipleship of Equals," in *Reconstructing Christian Theology*, ed. Rebecca S. Chopp and Mark Lewis Taylor (Minneapolis: Fortress Press, 1994), 90–91.

8. Ibid., 91.

9. McGrath, *Christian Theology*, 153.

10. George Stroup, "Revelation," in *Christian Theology: An Introduction to Its Traditions and Tasks*, rev. ed., ed. Peter C. Hodgson and Robert H. King (Minneapolis: Fortress Press, 1994), 116.

11. Ibid., 116–17.

12. Ibid., 137–38.

13. Friedrich Schleiermacher, *The Christian Faith*, ed. H. R. MacKintosh and J. S. Stewart (Edinburgh: T&T Clark, 1989), § 4, p. 12.

Chapter 4

What Do We Believe?

In the previous chapters, you arrived at the banks of the stream we call Christian theology. You have taken a quick tour of the flow of theological movements and activity down through the centuries, observing some of the twists and turns of these turbulent waters. Then you began to construct a raft that might help you travel along the stream of theology, piecing together the sources, methods, and approaches to theology. Significantly, you also began to think about your own starting point and sources for doing theology, since each of us must develop our own credo, or thoughtful understanding of what we believe. But all of that work, while important, is merely preliminary to the life that teems within these waters: our doctrines or teachings of the faith. Often we speak of the content of the Christian faith as a way of naming all of our theological concerns, our doctrines, our teachings. In this chapter, we examine the content of the Christian faith—though in a general and incomplete manner—so that you might begin to articulate, consciously and deliberatively, where you stand within the stream.

As you might expect, there is no one universally accepted set of beliefs or teachings held by all Christians. But we can turn to a skeletal framework that yields the common beliefs shared by most Christians—a starting point from which we diverge through deeper reflection and considerations. The basic outline of what Christians believe is found in the church's creeds, those statements of faith hammered out at the councils of the early church. The Apostles' Creed is most commonly used among Protestants, but the

Nicene Creed also provides a good starting point for theological engagement. It might be helpful to pause here and recite the Apostles' or Nicene Creed aloud. Listen to the shape of the words, and pay attention to the structure of the Apostles' Creed printed below as an example.

The Apostles' Creed

> I believe in God, the Father almighty,
>> creator of heaven and earth.
> I believe in Jesus Christ, his only Son, our Lord,
>> who was conceived by the Holy Spirit,
>> born of the Virgin Mary,
>> suffered under Pontius Pilate,
>> was crucified, died, and was buried;
>> he descended into hell.
>> On the third day he rose again;
>> he ascended into heaven,
>> he is seated at the right hand of the Father,
>> and he will come to judge the living and the dead.
> I believe in the Holy Spirit,
>> the holy catholic Church,
>> the communion of saints,
>> the forgiveness of sins,
>> the resurrection of the body,
>> and the life everlasting.
>> Amen.

Is there anything significant in the ordering of the faith claims? Are there beliefs that you would raise questions about? Every time the church or an individual recites a creed, each reciter has taken the first step in doing theology, though often it is done as an embedded rather than deliberative theological act. How many times have you recited this Apostles' Creed, knowing the words by heart, but not consciously considering their meaning?

Now go online and use a search engine to find an introduction to theology textbook (you will find a number of possibilities at the end of this chapter). Websites where you can purchase books will often provide you with a free glimpse inside, enabling you to review the table of contents. You might also borrow a theology textbook from a pastor, a seminarian, or the library. In either case, make sure it is an introduction to systematic theology. Turn to the table of contents, and read through it with some care. Do you see a resemblance to the creeds? While few theology textbooks follow the Apostles' or Nicene Creed exactly, you should still be able to discern a basic pattern to the teachings of the Christian faith. Check a second textbook in order to confirm this statement.

All theology textbooks will cover the same broad set of doctrinal concerns. These usually include preliminaries such as method and sources (prolegomena), God, Jesus Christ (Christology and soteriology), the Holy Spirit (pneumatology), humanity (theological anthropology), the church (ecclesiology), and the last things (eschatology). As you might expect, each doctrine has various theological considerations associated with it which deepen, expand, and complicate that teaching. For example, the doctrine of God will usually include not only questions of God's nature, but also the Trinity, creation, providence, theodicy, and other topics. Of course, how we explain and develop the detailed theological accounts within each doctrine varies by Christian tradition, denomination, and even era, which is why we do not have one common systematic theology textbook for all Christians in all times and places.

This diversity of interpretations and the intricacies of each doctrine mean that in this short book we cannot examine all the trajectories and different theological positions in detail. It is not my intention to direct you toward what I think are the "right" teachings or to impose my personal beliefs upon you. That would do you, the reader, a great disservice, since the goal of studying theology is to enable you to articulate your beliefs within the context of the communities of faith to which you belong, as well as to recognize differences that exist in our expressions and articulations of the faith. As a result, the pages that follow will emphasize two things. First, I want to help you grasp the basic contours of the broader doctrines and the key questions or concerns within each doctrine. The goal is to provide you with a sense of the points for further study and reflection, but the details of each doctrine are beyond the scope of this volume. Second, in doing so, I hope to encourage your deliberative reflection around questions that pastors often face from their congregations or must wrestle with in sermons, Bible studies, and pastoral situations. Remember our previous discussion of the problems related to asserting that everything is "God's will"? The basic doctrinal loci of the Christian faith should enable us to reflect more carefully and fully on such vital questions. So with this in mind, let's dive into the stream and begin to swim around in these swiftly moving and life-giving waters.

Most theology textbooks begin with the doctrine of God—a pattern we will follow here. But we could begin with any doctrine, because the content of the Christian faith is interrelated, and one doctrine leads to and is connected to the others. In Jürgen Moltmann's theology, especially his early theology, for example, the starting point is eschatology, or the notion that in the resurrection of Jesus Christ we find hope, which orients us toward God's promised future and our present mission in the world. Hope draws us forward toward God's good future. Thus, if he were to write a one-volume systematic theology, it might well begin with a chapter on eschatology as the focal point for how we do and enter into theological discourse. Depending upon the starting point or approach taken by a theologian, the order of the chapters might differ, but the same content would be presented. If you are a creative thinker, you might want to consider where you would want to begin your own theology and why that would be your focal or entry point. For our purposes, we will follow a more traditional order that approximates the Apostles' Creed.

I Believe in God

As we mentioned in chapter 1, the entirety of the study of the Christian faith begins and ends with God. We think of *God* as a name for the ultimate reality or divine being, though *God* is actually symbolic language. A symbol is something that both points to and participates in something else. For

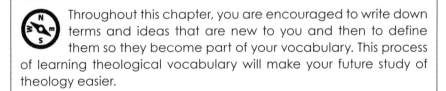

Throughout this chapter, you are encouraged to write down terms and ideas that are new to you and then to define them so they become part of your vocabulary. This process of learning theological vocabulary will make your future study of theology easier.

example, a nation's flag is a symbol, as it points to that nation, but also is deeply woven into the identity of the people. A symbol is contrasted with a sign, which simply points to something else. Take, for example, a stop sign.

It points toward the action the driver must take but does not participate in or carry meaning beyond that momentary action. Thus, when we speak of this word, *God*, as being symbolic, we do not diminish the divine reality but instead acknowledge our finitude in trying to name the fullness of the divine. God is not really the given name of the divine, but the symbol we use to point to and convey the meaning of the One we recognize as ultimate.

Recognizing that God is the symbol we use for the divine begins to awaken our minds and spirits to think more deeply and carefully about the subject of our faith. Suppose for a moment that you are on an airplane or in a coffee shop and a stranger sitting next to you sees that you're reading this book. The stranger asks what you are reading, and you explain that it is an introduction to the study of God and the life of faith, to what Christians believe. Then the stranger says, "I'm a scientist and believe in hard data," and he asks you this question: "Who is this God? Why should anyone believe in this unseen being? What makes God worthy of study or devotion or worship?" So, how would you begin to respond to the stranger? I imagine many would offer two basic responses. First, that God is love. But unless we are able to explain that God's love is of a different nature than human love, and what it means when we claim that God is love, our answer might not be very satisfying to the stranger. Second, we might respond with a claim that God is the creator of everything and the source of our salvation. But how will we make the idea of creation meaningful to a scientifically oriented mind? And how would we describe salvation to this person? If we simply say it is the promise of heaven, that answer will likely fall on deaf ears, as a concept that seems irrelevant or silly to many people today.

To answer well the question of who God is and why we care about and are devoted to God, we ourselves need to begin by asking questions and learning as much as possible about God. Theology, at heart, is a discipline of asking questions. The more you learn about God and the life of faith, the more questions you will have. It seems paradoxical. You would expect to have more answers. Of course, you do have more knowledge or understanding, but the reality of God is such that the more we ask and begin to understand, the more questions we are likely to have, and the more we will be humbled and in awe of this One we call God. Don't worry; God can stand up to our scrutiny and questions. After all, if we believe that God created human beings, then it is surely the case that God intends for us to use our minds to question and to learn.

In considering the doctrine of God, traditional theology will often begin with questions about the nature and attributes or characteristics of God. Ask yourself what you know about the nature of God; perhaps write down a list of attributes as a starting point. Then, as we go along, you can add to that list and begin to expand your understanding of who God is. But as you do so, you might find yourself wondering how we know anything about God. As we discussed in chapter 3, Christians have generally believed that we can know something of God through nature (general revelation), but our most intimate knowledge of God comes through special revelation and, in particular, through the life and teachings of Jesus of Nazareth, who is the Christ. Thus, we might begin by asking ourselves what we know about God from the scriptural witnesses.

There are, of course, a variety of biblical witnesses and a range of attributes ascribed to God, but there is no systematic accounting or comprehensive statement of who God is. Moses' encounter with the burning bush provides a starting point by reminding us that God will be who God will be (Exod. 3:14). Throughout our discussion of the doctrine of God, it will be

 Spend some time considering the qualities that the biblical witnesses ascribe to God.

helpful to keep in mind this divine excess that overflows our human capacities to know in full. The Bible tells us that God is creative, just, righteous, steadfast, loving, compassionate, and jealous, among other qualities. If we are reading carefully, we also would find that God is vindictive at times and sends the people of Israel to kill other peoples in battle. In both cases—whether the attributes are positive or seem less than divine—we are left to interpret the biblical witnesses and to confront our human limitations in fully understanding the nature of God. As human beings, we can only use our own frames of reference to interpret these claims to the nature of God. We can never know God in God's self.

Intellectually, there are three basic ways to approach our knowledge of these attributes, as first proposed by Thomas Aquinas. First, is the *via negativa* (the way of negation), by which we are able to look at all the imperfections of the created world in order to assess what God is not or to assign to

God the opposite quality. Thus, we are able to claim that God is not finite (e.g., *in*-finite). God is not arbitrary and capricious. God is not subject to decay and death. You can add to this list other qualities by way of negation. Second, we engage what is known as the *via causalitatis*, which means "the way of causality," or the idea that God is the cause or source of all things such as wisdom or goodness. The third approach, *via eminentiae* (the way of eminence), suggests that the perfections of the world can be attributed to God in a higher or more perfect sense (e.g., *all*-powerful or omnipotent), though remember that we should not assume God is simply quantitatively more of any attribute we observe in human beings. Some attributes of God might be considered as internal to God in God's self (e.g., perfection or unity), while others might be understood in relation to the world (e.g., freedom or mercy).

Thus, even though we have a tendency to speak of God as a "being," God is not a being in the sense of any other being that we know or can imagine. The character of God differs fundamentally from that of created beings, and for this reason, Paul Tillich used the phrases "Being Itself" and "the Ground of Being" to refer to this absolute distinction between God and all else. The classical formulation of God's existence, Anselm's ontological argument, points toward this fundamental distinction when he claims in Chapter II of his *Proslogium*, "Thou art a being than which nothing greater can be conceived." Though Anselm uses the terminology of God as "a being," he also suggests that our notion of this "being" is at the furthest reaches of our intellect and reason. Anselm's point is to prove the existence of God by means of a complex logic characteristic of the Scholastic theologians. Still, his ontological argument is helpful in identifying the distinctiveness of the "being-ness" of God.

But how does God relate to the world and to human beings? If a person is a deist, he or she believes that God set the world in motion but is no longer involved in its ongoing development and existence. Usually, we use the analogy of a clockmaker winding up the clock and then leaving it to run on its own. In other words, for deists, nothing that happens should be attributed to God's will or providence or agency. But most Christians are theists, in that we believe in the relationship of God to the created order. How much "control" God exerts over the creation is a matter of debate. If we believe that God determines absolutely everything that happens, then it is reasonable to claim that anything and everything is "God's will." If we hold a position in which God is involved in the world but does not dictate each moment and, in fact, gives us free will, then ascribing everything to "God's will" is meaningless and perhaps lazy thinking. We can do better if we want to communicate to others about the God we worship and serve.

Two terms commonly characterize the way in which God relates to and is present to the world: *transcendence* and *immanence*. God's transcendence denotes, in the language of Karl Barth, God's "wholly otherness." Transcendence suggests that God is set apart from the created order and is inaccessible to the human mind and senses. God is not found in human experience. God transcends our experience. God is shrouded in mystery, and the divine is unknowable and unapproachable, which might be reflected in the first creation story in Gen. 1:1—2:3. Sometimes Christians will behave as if they know God's will or truth with absolute certainty. Yet the transcendence of God reminds us that we are never in possession of the full truth, will, knowledge, or presence of God. God is removed and at a distance from human beings. Transcendence also relates to God's sovereignty or the notion that God has the final word or governs the universe and all that is within it. Traditionally, theists have stressed the otherness of God. Some theists so emphasize transcendence, or the distinction between God and all created things, that they virtually eliminate any sense of God's presence or relationship to the world.

Yet, simultaneously, we believe God is present to us and active within the cosmos. The word we use is immanence (not to be confused with imminence). God is immanent within the created order, in time and space, though not in physical form (except, of course, for the historical point of the incarnation in Jesus of Nazareth). Some interpreters suggest that God's immanence is highlighted in the second creation story in Gen. 2:4b—3:24. Immanence means that we can speak of God being with us and never leaving us alone or "orphaned" (John 14:18). Two clarifications should be made here about how God is present in the world. Pantheism argues that God and the natural world or universe are identical or equated, which might be considered the extreme form of immanence. God is utterly and completely present to and in the created world; the created order is God's very self. Therefore, pantheists eliminate the possibility of transcendence. The concept of panentheism goes in a different direction, claiming a middle ground in which God is present yet not equated with the creation. It neither isolates God from the world in stressing transcendence nor identifies or equates God with the world in stressing immanence. Thus, panentheism emphasizes the relationship between God and the created order. Sallie McFague and process theologians, among others, have engaged and developed notions of panentheism in contemporary theology, though critics have charged them with not taking transcendence seriously enough. Nonetheless, theology wrestles with the transcendence and immanence of God and generally seeks to find a balance between the two concepts. Where would you locate yourself among these options? How do you believe God relates to the created order?

There is a second way to engage this idea of the relationality of God, and that is through the doctrine of the Trinity. The biblical witnesses and the early Christians in their practices, such as the baptismal formula, accepted the divinity of God, Jesus Christ, and the Holy Spirit but had to clarify how we can claim to be monotheistic and yet distinguish three forms in

 Reflect upon other metaphors you might use to explain the mystery of the Trinity.

which the divine is known. The classical formulation is that God is of one substance (*ousia*) in three persons (*hypostases*). This doctrine of the Trinity is at the heart of the mystery of God's self-revelation. One analogy that may help us understand the Trinitarian formulation is the physical matter we know as H_2O, which can take the form of ice, water, and steam yet remains fundamentally the same chemical substance. Of course, we remember that all metaphors or analogies break down at some point; obviously, God is not physical matter with a molecular structure. But the imagery may be helpful in conceptualizing the Trinity as one substance expressed in three persons.

Typically, the relationality of the Trinity is further distinguished in the language of the *immanent or essential Trinity* and the *economic Trinity*. The immanent or essential Trinity refers to the interrelationship of the three persons of God within God's self, which remains hidden to us. We are unable to know who God is within God's self (the language used to refer to God's own being is God *in se*), traditionally understood as unchanging, though theologians have often debated whether God, in fact, can and does change. Here the term *perichoresis*, or the "mutual indwelling," of the three persons is sometimes used to describe the interrelationship of the three persons. There is, in the words of Saint Augustine, a "society of love" or a mutual indwelling within God, a way of sharing in the "life" of each person of the Godhead. More recently, liberation theologians have drawn on the concept of the equality and mutuality of the three "persons" of God to suggest it provides an appropriate model for human communities. Still, we must recognize that even as theologians posit such mutual indwelling, we have no way of actually confirming who God is *in se*.

Of great importance to the Christian faith is our belief that God has chosen to reveal God's self in the form of three persons traditionally named as God the Father, Jesus Christ the Son, and the Holy Spirit (or Holy Ghost in the past). This is the economic Trinity or the way in which God has been made known in relationship to the world. The word *economic* comes from the Greek word *oikonomikos*, referring to the management of a household or the organizing of a system. In the Christian context, *economic* takes on the sense of God's work in the process of salvation unfolding in history. In the economic trinity, viewed from the perspective of the human creatures who are the object of God's work of salvation, the way God is revealed has changed over the course of salvation history. Consider the incarnation and Jesus' sending of the Holy Spirit, which appear to human history as new expressions (though, of course, the Spirit is present in the Hebrew Scriptures and interpreters have considered those early witnesses to also point to Jesus Christ). In an oversimplification, the economic Trinity is about the way God relates to the world and the work God is doing in history on behalf of the redemption and reconciliation of the whole of creation. Notice that in the working of the Trinity in the world, the emphasis is placed upon salvation history and the relationship of the Triune God to the reconciliation of the whole of creation. This is not an individualistic concept in which God is concerned with *my* salvation, but rather, God is at work throughout human history for the sake of the healing and wholeness of the cosmos.

Now, when we claim that God as known in the economic Trinity is at work on behalf of the whole of creation, we are forced to wrestle with the problem of evil, or *theodicy* in theological terms. Theodicy is one of the thorniest theological issues we will ever encounter. In contemporary terms, the question might be, Why do bad things happen to good people? Here again, we encounter that often forwarded claim to "God's will" as the answer to difficult questions. But "God's will" is a hugely problematic claim in the face of evil. Let's begin by defining evil. According to Langdon Gilkey, evil can be defined as "that which thwarts continuously and seriously the potential goodness of creation, destroying alike its intelligibility and meaning and making life as we experience it so threatening, so full of sorrow,

 Familiarize yourself with this formula that expresses the problem of evil.

suffering, and apparent pointlessness."[1] Evil, by nature, is opposed to God; it is a perversion of the goodness of creation and creatures. Thus, when we ascribe everything to God, we are claiming that God has evil motives or that we simply do not understand the goodness that exists within what we view as evil. Traditionally, the problem of evil is articulated in a simple formula: If God is good and God is omnipotent, then how can evil exist? Stated differently, if there is evil, either God is not good or God is not all-powerful. Yet most Christians believe that God is both good and omnipotent.

As you might imagine, answers to theodicy have been posited down through the ages. For Irenaeus, the presence of evil in the world serves a catechetical function; its purpose is to enable spiritual growth and maturity, teaching us about righteousness. In the contemporary era, process theologians have taken this notion of learning the difference between good and evil and have suggested that God is self-limiting and works by means of persuasion rather than coercion.[2] We find that in the traditional understanding, it is not that God lacks goodness or power, but rather the presence of evil can be attributed to God's decision to give human beings free will to choose the good and thereby advance as human beings and as communities. But considering the presence of evil as an opportunity to learn and mature is problematic and often criticized in the light of genocide, weapons of mass destruction, and brutal acts of terrorism and violence. Surely there would be better ways to learn what is good than suffering through such atrocities.

Sometimes Christians have tried to respond to the problem of evil with a dualistic answer: matter is evil and spirit is good. Manichaeism held this position, and this idea reappears in different forms throughout Christian history. Early on, Saint Augustine rejected this dualistic approach (after a brief foray into Manichaeism himself) and argued that God's creation was deemed "good" in the beginning. Thus, the material, physical world cannot be evil in itself. Rather, God's decision to allow human beings free will meant that they could and did choose evil. It was through the actions of the human creature that evil entered the world. Yet because this leaves open the question of how evil could even be a choice, Augustine opined that Satan was the source of this possibility, and the first humans, through their disobedience, opened the door to evil. Yet once again, this leads to a question without a satisfactory answer: Who made Satan? Where did he originate? For Augustine, Satan was a fallen angel, created out of God's goodness, but in wanting to be like God, he disobeyed, and thus evil entered into existence. Yet this does not resolve the intellectual dilemma, as we have no answer for how a good angel could turn evil. Although Augustine's response to the problem of evil falls short of a full explanation, it has often been the standard response, especially in the murky figure of Satan as the real source of evil, thereby separating evil from God's goodness and omnipotence. In any case, theodicy continues to be an important concern among Christians and a subject raised by those who question the existence of God.

When we speak of evil and the problem of evil, it is also important to distinguish between natural and moral evil. Natural evil refers to the suffering that arises from natural processes, such as a tornado, flood, or disease like cancer with no known cause of origin. Clearly, there is a terribly destructive dimension to the natural order. It has been proposed traditionally that creation fell when the human creature fell and shall be restored to good order when humanity is redeemed and reconciled to God. Such a response does not fully answer all the questions we might have about natural evil. Nor do we have complete understanding of moral evil, which

 Distinguish between moral and natural evil, and think about other categories of actions or events that would fall within each type of evil.

is the suffering and destruction that arises from free will, out of the freedom human beings have to choose and act either toward the self or aimed at others. The problems previously mentioned, such as genocide and terrorism, fall into this category. So, too, do bullying, white-collar crime that wipes out the savings of middle-class investors, and often-preventable diseases that arise out of bad choices and reckless behavior. Moral evil can be seen to relate to sin, disobedience, or turning away from God. In either case, whether natural or moral in origin, the presence of evil persists. How comfortable are you, in light of what we have now considered, with the idea that everything is God's will?

Before we leave this brief introduction to the doctrine of God, there is at least one more consideration deserving our attention. It is the doctrine of creation. Based upon the Genesis accounts of creation, several theological concepts are indicated. First is the notion of creation *ex nihilo*, which means creation "out of nothing." There was not some preexistent matter, which God then formed. The creation did not emanate from God—as Greek philosophy had posited—but out of nothingness. The idea of nothing is hard for us to grasp. When you ask your friend, "What are you doing?" and she answers, "Nothing," she is still doing something.

While we simply cannot grasp the idea of nothingness, creation *ex nihilo* suggests at least two things for Christians. First, it is a historical claim. Our salvation history has a beginning point and, we believe, an ending point in which the fallen creation will be restored. For Dietrich Bonhoeffer, creation is a boundary which the human creature is incapable of thinking beyond. It is part and parcel of our finitude to live in the middle, between the beginning and the end. Second, we claim that in the act of creation, God ordered and organized the cosmos. As we mentioned previously, all of creation is orderly and reliable; for example, we know that the sun will rise and set in a predictable manner and that living things age, rather than growing younger as in the movie *The Curious Case of Benjamin Button*. Thus, everything that exists is a result of God's creative activity and agency. We believe that God was not compelled to create anything, but did so out of God's goodness and free choice. God does not depend upon anything created, though we acknowledge that the creation depends upon God's continued preservation of all things. Though evil exists and we might claim the world is fallen, it nevertheless does not cease to possess the contours of the original goodness in which it was made, nor does it ever cease to be that which is created.

This understanding of creation is often contested by modern science, as it considers the Christian concept of creation to be incompatible with scientific knowledge that is gained through observation, replicable testing, and data collection. Yet there is virtually nothing associated with the life of faith or the doctrine of creation that can be validated according to scientific principles. Today there are a number of theologians who are working to bridge the divide between faith and science and to demonstrate their compatibility. John Polkinghorne, for example, has argued that while science believes evolution or *creatio continua* (continuous creation) is opposed to traditional Christian doctrine, in actuality God respects the processes put into place at the creation, and thus evolution can be validated within the theological understanding of Christians. Admittedly, some Christians uphold a fundamentalist and literal interpretation of Scripture, which cannot be reconciled with scientific knowledge. But for most Christians who understand the interpretive nature of the scriptural witnesses, science can prove to be an engaging dialogue partner. Even so, one of the challenges Christians face in the contemporary age is the many questions people raise about the existence of God and reliable knowledge of the divine reality. This is a central task for Christian apologetics in the twenty-first century.

There is so much more, infinitely more, we could say about the doctrine of God: God's nature and attributes, the relationship of God to the created order, the problem of evil, the concept of creation, grace, impassibility (the idea of whether God can suffer), and so on. This brief introduction is intended only to begin your journey into understanding who God is and how God is at work in history. Yet at this point, you might wish to pause and make some notes on what you believe about God. You might also indicate what new insights you have gained over the course of these few pages. How would you now answer the scientifically minded person beside you on the airplane? What are the questions that continue to capture your interest, and what do you want to study in greater depth? Remember, theology—like faith itself—is a journey of discovery, and as you enter into seminary, carry these questions with you and let your mind and spirit be expanded and enriched. But don't forget that the more you learn about God, the more questions you will inevitably have.

I Believe in Jesus Christ

When we think of our faith and what it means to be a Christian, we automatically turn to the significance of Jesus Christ. We are concerned with who he is and what he does, as well as how we should follow and live out his example. Clearly, the doctrine of Jesus Christ is at the center or the heart of the Christian faith. Our understanding of who Jesus Christ is and what he does, the person and the work, Christology and soteriology, needs to be deeply examined and carefully expressed. Thus, as we turn to our teachings about Jesus Christ, we are faced with the impossibility of doing this doctrine justice in a few short pages. Our strategy, then, is first to consider the biblical witnesses to Jesus. Second, we will touch briefly on the theological debates around Jesus Christ in the early church, which set the foundation for our christological understanding. Third, we will consider the meaning of the incarnation, crucifixion, and resurrection of Jesus Christ, which will include considerations of his work, or soteriology.

So, to begin, who do you say that Jesus Christ is? How do you understand who he is and what he has accomplished on behalf of the world, and how would you explain that to others? And who is Jesus Christ for us *today*? Most Christians talk quite a bit about Jesus. Many pray to Jesus. The gospels share the good news of Jesus Christ. Yet at times, our conceptions about Jesus Christ are shallow, misty renderings of this one who is central to our faith. In this section, we want to open up new pathways into the person and work of Jesus Christ to see if our vision might grow sharper.

Imagine you are in mission with your church, helping to build a Habitat for Humanity house alongside other groups from the community. As you and another person are painting walls inside the house, you begin a conversation with the woman beside you. She is not a person of faith, and she asks you how a man who was a good teacher two thousand years ago could now be worshipped as the Savior. While she thinks Jesus of Nazareth was a good, moral person with wisdom, she has a hard time with the notion that he could be God. How would you begin to respond? Surely, you couldn't just say, "The Bible tells me so, and I believe it." That would be an unsatisfying answer to this woman. So then, how did Christians come to this understanding of Jesus? Could you help her see how the tradition and the biblical witnesses have woven together through the centuries to enable our belief? Could you express to her who Jesus Christ is for us today, in this day and age, and why he is central to your life? Let's look at the doctrine of Jesus Christ with an eye toward your ability to share a carefully crafted answer about Jesus Christ, the center of our faith.

There is good reason to begin with this doctrine's biblical and historical basis—the witnesses to the life of Jesus of Nazareth, to whom the New

Testament, particularly the gospels, bear witness and to whom the church has sought to be faithful through the centuries. In the person of Jesus and our access to him through these witnesses, we are provided with the fullest revelation of who God is and who we are created to be. Without this starting point, we would be limited in our ability to articulate anything about our Christian faith. This starting point of the testimony of Scripture and tradition in developing the doctrine of Jesus Christ also provides us with an example of how these two primary sources are applied in the practice of theological reflection.

Christology begins with the New Testament. Before there were church councils and various discussions *about* Jesus Christ, there were witnesses *to* his life, death, and resurrection. Certainly, no witness provides a perfectly accurate account, and each witness has a particular lens through which he or she views the historical life. Each witness tells the story in a particular way in order to emphasize specific aspects of what has been revealed in Jesus Christ in order to have the greatest impact upon his or her intended audience. So, we should realize that the scriptural testimony is already presenting us with various theological interpretations. There is no one biblical Christology, but various accounts, which is why it has been suggested that the biblical witnesses are more like an oil painting than a photograph of Jesus. The gospels are not intended to be historical records but to offer the good news of Jesus Christ pieced together from the oral accounts that had circulated over the decades before the gospels were recorded. Thus, from the beginning, Christians have sought to understand the person and work of Jesus Christ, but there has never been unanimity in expressing these concerns. This is also to say that Christians have always been attentive to the question, Who is Jesus Christ for us today?

The New Testament is our primary source for Christology, but it is meaningful only within the context of the Hebrew Scriptures. *Christ* is, of course, the Greek translation of the Hebrew word *mashiah*, or messiah. *Messiah* means someone who has been anointed, and the Messiah was associated with the eschatological expectations of Israel. Although many people could be anointed—kings, priests, prophets—the coming Messiah was to be a king like David, who would restore the greatness of Israel. This Messiah was to be a political, military leader. But Jesus did not fulfill these expectations, since his battles were not military ones and he rejected being considered a "king." Jesus reached out to those whom society despised and marginalized, he challenged the authorities of his day, and he questioned their practices. No wonder the political and religious leaders of his day felt threatened by him and turned against his message. Thus, when the New Testament points to Jesus as the Messiah, a process is under way of redefining the meaning of *Messiah* or *Christ*. In 1 Cor. 15:3, Paul uses the word *Christ* simply as a reference to Jesus, implying that, by definition, who he is and what he does are the true meaning of the Messiah. If nothing else, we should be reminded to be careful in expressing our own expectations about Jesus who is the Christ.

Other titles present in the New Testament witnesses include Son of God and Son of Man, Lord, and Rabbi. Each of these biblical titles offers some insight into the person of Jesus Christ. Neither Son of God nor Son of Man was a title given only to Jesus, as in Hebrew (*ben*) or Aramaic (*bar*), *son* meant "belonging to." This usage might be indicated by Mark 2:27, 28 or in Exod. 4:22, when Israel is declared to be God's firstborn "son," though

Spend some time thinking about the titles used in reference to Jesus Christ and the way they work together to form an understanding of who he is.

this language applied to Jesus will point theologians toward the recognition of Jesus as fully human and fully divine. *Lord* is a title that referred to God, Yahweh, in the Hebrew Scriptures, and the confession that "Jesus is Lord" (Rom. 10:9) becomes one of the earliest christological confessions. We can see that the New Testament begins to point toward one of the fundamental doctrinal statements about Jesus, though it will be the early second century before the church affirms the equality of Jesus with God. Finally, we should remember that Jesus was a rabbi, a teacher of Israel, having studied the law in the temple. But as his ministry unfolds, his teachings have the authority not of the priests, scribes, and prophets, but of God. In sum, the ways in which the New Testament writers refer to Jesus become a key source of information and deliberation over the identity of Jesus Christ. These biblical witnesses are providing answers to the question, Who is Jesus Christ?

But of course, the titles applied to Jesus are only one source of understanding who he is. The writings of Paul also are an important theological basis for our doctrine of Jesus Christ, though which letters are authentically

Paul's is a matter of debate among New Testament scholars. Nonetheless, as the earliest documents about Jesus, Paul's letters are especially important in the development of Christology, and we can discern a few basic themes they address. These themes are Jesus' humanity, divinity, crucifixion, resurrection, and finally *parousia*, or expected return.

Paul expresses clearly that Jesus existed as a human being, "born of a woman, born under the law" (Gal. 4:4) and that he "descended from David according to the flesh" (Rom. 1:3). Paul also contrasts the sin of the one man, Adam, with the gift of righteousness through the one man, Jesus Christ (Rom. 5:12-21). At the same time as Paul is pointing toward the humanity of Jesus, he is also confessing Jesus' divinity. As we noted previously, in Rom. 10:9 we find the earliest christological confession that "Jesus is Lord" and the source of our salvation. In 1 Cor. 16:22, we encounter the phrase *maranatha*, which can be read in two different ways. When Paul wrote his letters, the Greek language used no paragraphing, spaces between words, or punctuation as we know it today, but simply one letter written after the other. To read Paul's original writing, then, requires us to make judgments about where to divide the letters into words and sentences. Most translations of the Bible will have small, superscript letters to indicate uncertainties in the reading of a text. In the case of this word, *maranatha*, we find that the Greek could be read in two distinct ways: (1) as *marana tha*, meaning "Our Lord, come!" or (2) as *maran atha*, which translates to "Our Lord has come!" I prefer to think that Paul intended to convey both meanings to suggest that Jesus has come and will come again, which is a reflection of his divine nature and purpose. Regardless of which way you might choose to interpret *maranatha*—and it requires us to make interpretive decisions—it is quite clear that Paul recognizes Jesus' lordship or that he is God.

Have you noted that Paul is reflecting theologically on the meaning of Jesus Christ? He is not providing a historical account of Jesus' life, death, and resurrection, but a theological statement of the meaning of Jesus for the lives of his followers. Paul is developing notions of Jesus as human and as God, but there is not yet present in his writings a fully developed doctrine of the two natures of Jesus. Nonetheless, his writings will form a crucial basis for later deliberations regarding the two natures of fully human, fully divine. As we continue with Paul's writings, you should notice how much we take for granted the meaning of his statements, though this clarity would not occur without centuries of church deliberations.

Paul's letters have much to say about the significance of the crucifixion. This act was not simply a mistaken execution, but an atonement or reconciliation for the sins of all humanity (Rom. 3:23-25). The sense of universal salvation for those who believe in Jesus is a crucial point in Paul's letters, since it means that Israel was no longer singled out as God's chosen people. In Rom. 10:12-13, Paul highlights that there is "no distinction between Jew and Greek," and "Everyone who calls on the name of the Lord shall be saved," which is a reinterpretation of the prophet Joel 2:32 in the context of Christ's crucifixion. For Paul, the cross not only is the source of salvation for all, but is a stumbling block for Jews and foolishness to Gentiles. We might say that the crucifixion did not seem like the expected answer for either tradition. This sense of the universality of the atonement is repeated in Gal. 3:27-28 and elsewhere in Paul's letters, thus suggesting an important emphasis of Paul's emerging Christology. The salvific function of the cross is not limited to certain people, places, times, or conditions, but offered to all. Of course, later interpreters will debate and define how the saving power of the cross works and what that offer to all means.

Hand-in-hand with the foolishness of the cross is the mystery of the resurrection, which stands as a second crucial emphasis in Paul's letters. He indicates that the atonement of the cross is not complete without the resurrection (1 Cor. 15:17), which overcomes death, the result of sin. For Paul, the resurrection is a promise and goal for those who are in Christ; it is the power of life (Phil. 3:10). The resurrection represents hope for those who take on the mind of Christ and join him in the sufferings of the world. But the resurrection has a present-future quality, an already-but-not-yet sense, as believers live with one foot in the kingdom of humanity and its brokenness and the other in the kingdom of God and its redemption. Christians are to await the return of Christ, who will complete the resurrection and the reconciliation of all things (1 Thess. 4:15-17). This tension of the work of Christ completed but not yet is a constant theme in Paul's writings.

Let's turn now to the Gospel of John and its high Christology (emphasizing his divinity) centered in the Word, the *Logos* of God. The Greek word *logos* has a rich history of usage and multiple meanings in the ancient world, beyond what we can examine here. Generally, it referred to the spoken word, as in God speaking creation into existence (the Hebrew word *debar* reflects this sensibility), and to inward thought or the life of the mind. In John, Jesus Christ is the *Logos*, the Word of God become flesh in both senses of the inward thought and the outward expression. John tells us that "in the beginning was the Word" (1:1), which signifies Christ's preexistence with God, rather than as a creation of God. Thus, John begins the process of identifying that the Word of God is fully present in Christ and accessible to those who believe in him.

We have considered some of the key christological ideas found in the letters of Paul and in the Gospel of John, in order to demonstrate how the Scriptures begin the task of theological reflection. But of course, even if we included all the writings of the New Testament, we would still lack a fully formed Christology. The incompleteness of and, at times, differences in the scriptural witnesses led to the rise of various interpretations, which created divisions and debates in the early church as the doctrine developed. As we turn to examining the role of tradition in developing our understanding of both the person and work of Jesus Christ, we need to keep this sense of uncertainty in mind and the resulting motivation for Christians to clarify or respond to challenges. One of the first challenges came from Marcion, who is best known for arguing that the God of the Old Testament and the God of Christ in the New Testament were, in fact, two different gods. Christologically, Marcion claimed that Jesus was not a true man and did not have a physical, material body—a position that was deemed heretical and led to his expulsion from the church.

There were Gnostics teaching spiritual redemption through knowledge, rather than a bodily resurrection. Gnostics believed that Jesus brought knowledge that allows for spiritual salvation and that he only appeared to be human—a heresy known as Docetism. Though Gnostics were deemed heretics, their teachings caused the church to examine its Christology more closely, to consider if Jesus was actually, fully human. Indeed, throughout the second and third centuries, there were debates about the meaning of Christ's work of salvation. The Gnostic position of sacred knowledge and spiritual salvation represents one position. A second view of Christ's nature and work is represented in Eastern Orthodoxy and articulates concerns for human *theosis*, or deification (union with God). A third early position viewed Jesus' work in terms of the forgiveness of sins or justification, which became the main soteriological thread in the West.

When the debates about the Trinity raged in the fourth century, Christology was one of the central concerns. How should Christians understand the relationship between God the Father and the Son? A number of solutions were offered. Some argued that Christ was a man who was adopted by God's spirit at baptism or at another time, which is known as an adoptionist Christology. Sabellius introduced a modalistic Christology, which suggested that there were successive—but not simultaneous—manifestations of the Father, then the Son, and finally the Holy Spirit. There arose a form of binitarian thinking, or a Spirit Christology which held there were only the Father and the Son-Spirit, thereby allowing a way for Jesus to be preexistent. This Spirit Christology forced the church to consider the relationship of Jesus Christ to the Holy Spirit as well. Finally, as previously mentioned, the *Logos* Christology emerged, locating the identity of Jesus Christ in the *Logos* (Word) and in the title Son of God. But the Son of God language led Arius to introduce the idea that Jesus was a creature, albeit the first among all creatures, but not God. Arianism was denounced at the first Council of Nicaea.

This brief and incomplete depiction of early christological debates suggests that there was never a clear, universally agreed upon idea of the nature or identity of Jesus Christ. It took centuries of debate and the Councils of Nicaea and Chalcedon among others to resolve the debate in favor of the two natures of Jesus Christ, fully divine and fully human, which we hold today. But even in our own time, many people continue to question and ask about the nature of Jesus Christ, which means we need to exercise care in recognizing that our beliefs may not be as rigidly fixed as some might think. After all, how do you explain one who is fully divine dying on the cross? That he only appeared to be human? That his humanity was emptied out at that point? That it is a paradox and central mystery of the Christian faith? In addition, we recognize the important task of making our theology and Christology meaningful in each day and age by articulating it anew for our own generation.

The classic Christology confirmed by the Council of Chalcedon continued through the Middle Ages, though theories of atonement came to the forefront. In other words, with the disputes about the nature of Jesus Christ more or less settled, the work of Jesus Christ came under increasing scrutiny. How is the crucifixion effective in the forgiveness of sins? How is it that we are reconciled to God through Christ's death on the cross? Does the problem lie in the powers of evil, which must be overcome? Is there something within the human being that must be changed? Why do we need the crucifixion anyway? The easiest way to remember the meaning of atonement is simply to divide the word into *at-one-ment* to represent the notion of reconciliation between God and humanity. The crucifixion, of course, is situated in the context of the Old Testament understanding of the

 As you read about these atonement theories, identify the strengths and weaknesses of each.

sacrificial system of Israel, in which to atone for one's sins, the high priest would offer a sacrifice to God. It is in this context that Jesus as the Lamb of God taking away the sins of the world begins to take on its meaning. Several theologians, including Anselm and Abelard, offered explanations about how the atonement actually works to provide justification (forgiveness) and restoration.

The prevailing theory in the early church has been called the *Christus Victor* or ransom theory of atonement. This theory holds that there is essentially a cosmic battle taking place between the good God and the evil forces of the world. It's a theme we see played out regularly in movies and literature such as the Harry Potter series of J. K. Rowling. This ransom theory suggests that humanity is in bondage to the forces of evil. When God was disguised in the form of a human, Jesus of Nazareth, these evil forces were tricked into seeing him as easy prey rather than God, which enabled Christ's death to defeat evil and free humanity from its grip. Jesus became the ransom for us. You can probably come up with a number of questions that make this theory seem less than adequate. For example, does this theory represent a form of Docetism in which Jesus only appears to be human? What about the fact that evil and sin continue to exist in our world? How, then, did the crucifixion defeat the forces of evil? And what about our own free will and our responsibility for choices we make? Does this cosmic battle suggest that we have no role in or responsibility for our actions? These are just some of the questions we might raise, and perhaps you can think of yet others that show the weaknesses in the ransom model. While this first model clearly demonstrates the sense of a cosmic drama between forces of good and evil, which seems true to our human experience, unsettled questions remain.

In the medieval era, Anselm proposed a second theory of atonement commonly referred to as the satisfaction theory, which is still widely held by many Christians. Essentially, this theory suggests that human beings have disobeyed God, and as a result, God must be satisfied (think of this as the payment of a debt). If the debt is not satisfied, then punishment is due. Because sin is endless and only God can provide satisfaction for humanity, God became human so that in Jesus' perfect obedience, the satisfaction due to God could be rendered, and human sins forgiven. In this theory, once again, we encounter unsettled questions. The logic of God satisfying God by giving God's self seems peculiar. Couldn't God just erase that debt? And isn't grace free and unconditional? What about the fact that God is love? Shouldn't a God who is love have a better way to restore humanity than violence and death? While many questions surround the satisfaction theory of atonement, this view takes seriously sin and its consequences, as well as the human inability to adequately atone for our misdeeds.

A third atonement theory, moral influence, was first put forth by Abelard. This theory takes seriously the notion that in Christ and the cross, God's love is displayed in such a dramatic and convincing manner that human beings are inspired to follow Jesus' example. This theory thus suggests that the atonement that takes place on the cross must be appropriated by faith if it is to be completed. Unlike the satisfaction theory, which requires the sacrifice of Jesus to fulfill the debt owed to God, the moral influence theory emphasizes the love of God and the human response to grace. The example provided by Jesus on the cross fundamentally changes something within us, and we are thus moved to live differently. Of course, we should also note that in the modern era, the moral influence theory tended to stress the humanity of Jesus as a good example and to promote the idea of human moral perfection through reason. Yet this theory also has its weaknesses. We might ask about the power of sin and whether moral influence is strong enough to break that grip. And what about the presence of evil in the world? Is a good example sufficient to counteract the reality of evil? Nonetheless, the emphasis on God's love in Jesus Christ is a compelling way to articulate the salvific work of Christ.

Ultimately, all atonement theories fall short in our understanding. Not long ago, I participated in a worship service at the Church of the Resurrection in Leawood, Kansas. In his sermon, Pastor Adam Hamilton brought to light atonement theories and then proposed that the cross should be thought of as poetry or art more than an intellectual and definitive theory. The work of the cross draws us in and speaks to our lives, but it remains an unsolved mystery. Christians believe that the death of Jesus Christ on the cross has the power to reconcile us to God and to one another. Of course, Jesus' final words in John 19:30, "It is finished," leave us with a question mark, for we recognize that we still live in a world in which sin and evil are pervasive. All is finished, yet it is not finished. Even those who try to follow Christ cannot always do the right thing or avoid suffering and pain. Death remains our destiny. Human nature has not yet been fully recreated. But these words and the cross hold before us the powerful promise that God has become flesh in Jesus in order that we might be forgiven, reconciled, and restored to right and radical relationship. Even so, we are left to reflect upon the cross—its foolishness as well as its incomprehensibility as the means of our forgiveness.

Having introduced the crucifixion, which is a central doctrine of the Christian faith, we now turn to an overview of the incarnation and the resurrection, since without the incarnation, the crucifixion lacks power, and without the resurrection, death is not overcome. Indeed, the church's highest holy days are those celebrating the incarnation (Christmas) and the resurrection (Easter). On the one side of the cross stands the doctrine of the incarnation in which we claim that the one God has become embodied in the world in Jesus Christ. The Gospel of John tells us that the Word became flesh and dwelt among us (1:14). The incarnation is a reality that must be taken on faith, for the idea that Jesus Christ could be fully human and at the same time fully divine is a paradox. There is no logical explanation, no way for human reason to make sense of this historical reality. Yet the incarnation tells us several important things about God and humanity. For one, the fact that God took on human flesh indicates that the material world, the body is not inherently bad or evil. Indeed, in the first creation story in Genesis chapter 1, God declares the creation and the human creature to be good. This claim is significant, given the number of theologies over the centuries that have denied or denigrated physicality and the human body. Further, when we consider atonement theories, clearly the incarnation represents the initial point at which the reconciliation of God and humanity occurs. In this one historical person and moment, God and humanity are in perfect and right relationship. Third, the incarnation suggests to us that our God is not a distant, uncaring one, but rather, God understands our lives and world intimately. Perhaps in your own reflection on the incarnation, you can think of other meaningful claims that can be made beyond the story we tell at Advent and Christmas about the child in the manger.

On the other side of the cross stands the resurrection, which is central to the gospels and the letters of Paul, and is the very heartbeat of Christian faith. While we often emphasize the cross, even wearing it as a symbol around our neck, the empty tomb breaks open the crucifixion by overcoming death and bringing new life and the promise of the new creation to all. Perhaps we should all be wearing empty tombs around our necks. The resurrection stands as the central symbol of hope in the face of the violence and brokenness of the world and our lives. When we speak of the resurrection, we are first and foremost referring to the resurrection of Jesus to life following his death on the cross at Calvary. The resurrection of Jesus is the central symbol of the Christian year, as every Sunday when the church gathers in worship, that worship is the celebration of a mini-Easter, a recognition that Jesus has conquered death and offered new life, abundant life. The resurrection stands before us as a constant reminder that death does not have the final word and that God is a God of life. The resurrection gives shape to our lives and our faith with its emphasis on the hope and promises of God. The resurrection also points to the new life given to believers when they accept the gift of faith. In a spiritual sense, we are resurrected, given new life, even though the physical resurrection, the resurrection of the body, remains as a distant hope. That notion of physical resurrection after death is, of course, shrouded in mystery. We do not know what we shall become, and of course, there is no historical evidence to which we can turn in order to substantiate the resurrection of Jesus Christ upon which we stake this belief. It is a claim we accept by faith. We hold fast to the claim of life beyond death, which gives us the hope and the strength to live fully and confidently.

As we approach the end of this introduction to the doctrine of Jesus Christ, we come full circle to the question, Who is Jesus Christ for us today? For most Christians, when asked this question of the identity of Jesus Christ, the answer will be the Son of God, the Messiah, the Savior, the Lord. Some might simply say that all we need to know is "Jesus loves me." If we return to the woman beside you at the Habitat for Humanity house, telling her, "Jesus loves you," probably won't answer her questions, though the love of Jesus Christ can be compelling in a world that often seems loveless. One of the unfortunate christological turns in recent decades has been the tendency to turn Jesus Christ into "my personal Lord and Savior," when the tradition has always emphasized that salvation is located within the church community and that right relationship is not simply about one person's reconciliation to God, but the interweaving of all believers in right relationship with God and one another. The modern mind-set with its individualistic emphasis has warped the communal depth of the meaning of Jesus Christ. This radical relationship or communal, even cosmic quality is a teaching that should be stressed as central to our Christology.

In response to your co-laborer on that Saturday afternoon, theology would also posit, traditionally, that salvation is the act of being saved from the consequences of sin, which are suffering and death, and the going to heaven, which is life after death. These are the marks of the crucifixion and resurrection. But salvation has a deeper meaning still, and in today's world, salvation expressed in traditional terms may not be as compelling as it once was. If we wish to speak meaningfully to this woman who is open to conversation, we might need to carefully choose our language and way of expressing who Jesus is and what he does. So how might we articulate the meaning of Christ's work of salvation, his crucifixion and resurrection, in ways that are faithful to Christian teaching and meaningful to contemporary ears?

To make a theological move toward relevance might begin with understanding the word *salvation* and its genesis. *Salvation* comes from the Latin *salvus*, meaning "well, safe, sound, unharmed, saved." The word has many nuances and is not simply translated into English as "saved," at least in

 You may wish to do further study on the word *salvation*, as well as the biblical concept of *shalom*, or peace.

the sense that is often bandied about among contemporary Christians. "Are you saved?" they ask, in what is often an oversimplification or soon leads to some comment about going to heaven. To speak of being well, safe, and sound leads us toward an understanding of wholeness that is supported by the biblical concept of *shalom*, or peace. Often we think of peace as the absence of conflict, but the biblical concept is one of healing and wholeness. It points toward the fullness of life. Thus, when the resurrected Jesus appears to the disciples, breathes on them, and says, "Peace be with you" (Luke 24:36; John 20:21, 26), he is offering them *shalom*, healing and wholeness. Here we encounter the most profound meaning of Jesus Christ and who he is and remains for us today: the one who brings healing and wholeness so that all human beings may receive abundant life, may be healed and whole in the here and now as well as the hereafter. The fullness of life is offered to us by Jesus Christ. So, then, who is Jesus Christ for us today? What would you tell the woman who seeks to know more?

I Believe in the Holy Spirit

Our doctrine of God is not complete until we have considered the Third Person of the Trinity, the Holy Spirit. Yet as feminist theologian Elizabeth Johnson has claimed, the doctrine of the Holy Spirit, or pneumatology, tends to be neglected in theological reflection, both historically and in the contemporary era. Even so, the Spirit (or Spirit-Sophia, as Johnson names the Third Person) is "nothing less than the mystery of God's personal engagement with the world."[3] More than that, says Johnson, "Forgetting the Spirit is not ignoring a faceless, shadowy third hypostasis but the mystery of God closer to us that we are to ourselves, drawing near and passing by in quickening, liberating compassion."[4] As we begin to engage the doctrine of the Holy Spirit, it is worth considering whether you have tended to forget the Holy Spirit, to emphasize Jesus and God, but not the Spirit in all its fullness. How have you known and spoken of this expression of God's very self? It is important to remember that the Holy Spirit is God, not a creation of or emanation from God. In our doctrine of the economic Trinity, the Holy Spirit represents one of the three ways that God has chosen to be made known and at work in our world. When we turn to the Scriptures, we readily find the Spirit's movement and presence in the world.

The Hebrew Scriptures first speak of the Spirit or *ruach* (wind, breath, spirit) in the creation narrative, as a "wind from God" that sweeps across the formless face of the waters as God begins to create the heavens and the earth (Gen. 1:2). The Spirit is also represented as breath (though the breathing of life into the earth creature, *adam*, is a different Hebrew word), an image that provides us with a sense of the Spirit's life-giving quality. From the very beginning, then, the Spirit is revealed in terms of God's power and enlivening presence. The *ruach* is found in Psalms and the prophets, usually referred to as the Spirit of God, and only in Ps. 51:11 and Isa. 63:10, 11 do we find the Hebrew writers speaking of the "holy" spirit. In the New Testament, the Greek work *pneuma* continues this trajectory of the Spirit as the power and life-giving presence of God. The Spirit again is revealed as the power of God and the giver of life at work in the world, bringing to reality the promised new creation, but also serving as comforter and advocate in the midst of this already-but-not-yet existence.

There are a variety of ways in which theologians have described the Holy Spirit, but these descriptions almost always point toward the Spirit's

 Make note of the work of the Holy Spirit as you read through this section.

work or mission among us in the world. This emphasis on the work of the Spirit makes sense, given that we cannot know God in God's self (the inner relationship of the immanent Trinity). In every case, the Spirit looms as a relational reality drawing us into the work and presence of God, as well as creating a bond among people of faith. Turning again to Elizabeth Johnson, the Holy Spirit's activities might be referred to as vivifying, renewing and empowering, and gracing.

To speak of the "vivifying" activity of the Holy Spirit, we are pointed toward its creative power in the sense of *creatio continua*, or ongoing, continuous creation. What a wonderful, descriptive word Johnson has chosen in her use of *vivifying*. To vivify is to give life, to animate, to make more vivid or, we might say, to make more fully alive. Johnson demonstrates how our language about God, well chosen, can deepen our understanding and add to our reflective engagement. In speaking about the Holy Spirit's work of vivification, we come to see that not only does God give life by means of the Spirit, but God offers the fullness of life, a sense of becoming more than merely a living being with the breath of life. Through the Holy Spirit, we are enabled to become fully alive, fully the people God created us to be: filled with love or holiness (the theological term for this process is *sanctification*), as well as compassion, kindness, justice, generosity, and so forth. To go one step further, in *The Spirit of Life*, Jürgen Moltmann argues that the Holy Spirit is the enlivening presence and power within Jesus Christ himself. By analogy, the work of the Holy Spirit creates in us a more Christ-like character, enabling us to become more fully human. This is, indeed, vivifying.

In Johnson's depiction, the second activity of the Holy Spirit is a "transforming energy" of renewal and empowerment in the face of the world's brokenness.[5] In other words, the Holy Spirit provides the power for renewing and recreating people, the earth, even political and economic systems. Of course, this is not to suggest that human beings can take a passive role in this process, but that the Holy Spirit provides the energy and direction so that we might engage in the process of God's mission in the world. We do not need to look far to see the brokenness of the world, its hatred, violence, and suffering. Many people feel fragmented, unmoored, and without a way to pull the scattered pieces of their lives into a meaningful and life-giving wholeness. For Christians, the source of this transformation, the glue if you will, is the Holy Spirit. Paul Tillich expressed well this notion of finding unity amid the brokenness of existence, by correlating the existential question of fragmentation and ambiguity with the theological answer of the Spirit. The Holy Spirit, God's transforming energy, brings together the shattered and scattered pieces of human life into a meaningful whole.

Johnson names the third function of the Holy Spirit as "gracing." Grace, of course, is the unmerited love of God which is freely given to us. That grace is the presence of God, ever with us, whether we are conscious of the Spirit's presence or not. But even more, we find that the gracing activity of the Spirit includes the giving of gifts. These are not material gifts, as might be proclaimed by a prosperity gospel in a false interpretation of the scriptural witnesses. Rather, the gifts of the Spirit are given for mutual upbuilding, for the sake of the community and its life in God. This gift giving is articulated by Paul in his First Letter to the Corinthians: "Now there are varieties of gifts, but the same Spirit; and there are varieties of services, but the same Lord; and there are varieties of activities, but it is the same God who activates all of them in everyone. To each is given the manifestation of the Spirit for the common good" (12:4-7). In this passage, we discover that the one body has many persons differently gifted by the Spirit, but each is an essential part of the whole. Indeed, it is the Spirit that chooses which gift is made manifest in which person and thus prevents anyone from boasting in his or her own capacities or from assuming a superior place by virtue of supposedly greater gifts. The gifting of the Spirit serves an equalizing purpose among the faithful, encouraging us to resist comparing ourselves and our contributions with others.

This gracing activity of the Holy Spirit is also seen in the "fruit of the Spirit" described in Gal. 5:22-26. Here again, the equalizing quality of the Holy Spirit comes to the forefront. The passage begins with an admonition to reject the desires of the flesh, which requires some care in order to prevent us from pitting the "flesh" against the "spirit" in a way that diminishes the goodness of God's created order in favor of a spiritualized interpretation. If we live in the presence of the Spirit's gracing activity, the Spirit will guide us into a life that manifests itself in expressions of love, joy, peace, patience, kindness, generosity, faithfulness, gentleness, and self-control. Another text that offers a glimpse of the fruit of the Spirit is Acts 2:43-47, in which we are told that "all who believed were together and had all things in common, they would sell their possessions and goods and distribute the proceeds to all, as any had need. Day by day, as they spent much time together in the temple, they broke bread at home and ate their food with glad and generous hearts, praising God and having the goodwill of all the people." In other words, when we open ourselves to the Spirit, we find that the life of God takes up residence within us, and this indwelling gifts us with Christ-like-ness.

While we can barely touch upon the Holy Spirit and its work or mission in this book, we will conclude with one additional, and significant, action: its birthing of the church, the community of believers. The book of Acts begins with the followers of Jesus receiving his command to wait for the coming of the Holy Spirit. The disciples seem committed to waiting, praying, and staying together. Then on the day of Pentecost, the sound "like the rush of a violent wind" fills the house, and the Spirit enables them to speak and hear in other languages. At Babel, God had "confused" their language, scattering the people into a state of disunity (Genesis 11), though, we might suggest, Babel also represents the development of the world's diversity, whose fragmentary quality finds its unity and oneness only in and through the giving of the Spirit at Pentecost. The Holy Spirit does not act so as to make all people the same, but instead to bring a sense of unity in the midst of diversity. Thus, the birth of the church at Pentecost provides us with this crucial insight that the goal of life in the Spirit is not sameness, but rather a unity and togetherness expressed in the midst of great diversity.

There is, of course, much more to be said about the church, which we will take up in the following section on ecclesiology.

I Believe in the Church

The church is really a rather peculiar entity. What other voluntary organization brings people together on a weekly basis, collects money from them, and then redistributes (ideally) that money to care for others? If merely seen from this perspective, it's no wonder the church is declining in our contemporary society, which is dominated by individualism and capitalistic aspirations. The church is, or should be, a distinctly counter-cultural reality. Yet at the same time, the church is located in the midst of the surrounding culture, facing all the same issues as the society. So what is the church? How would you begin to talk about why you believe in the value and validity of the church, and how would you do so in a way that distinguishes it from other groups and organizations? No doubt, there is a great need to provide meaningful expressions of the church to a society that increasingly considers itself "spiritual but not religious." So how would you begin to explain the church and your commitment to this peculiar institution to someone who feels that all institutions are suspect, self-serving, and unworthy of his or her participation? This question is an important one in today's society, and any Christian, lay or clergy, should have a thoughtful response to offer.

What, then, does it mean to say we believe in the church? On the one hand, the church is an institution of human making, beset with all the problems faced by any human institution. It should not surprise us, then, that people will view the church as hypocritical, unloving at times, and judgmental. The church is all those things and more. Centuries ago, Saint Augustine answered similar charges with his claim that the church is a hospital for sinners. The church remains a reflection of the world's brokenness. But on the other hand, the church is also a mystical, spiritual community in which the new creation, reconciliation and restoration, is actually present, if only in part. The church, as a spiritual reality, has the power to participate in the transformation of the world. We should never lose sight of this both-and character of the church. So with this tension in mind, let's begin to unpack the meaning and substance of the church, the doctrine of ecclesiology.

The roots of the church as a community of God's people are found in the Hebrew Scriptures. The Old Testament is where our biblical understanding of the church originates, as an institution of people who gather together

 If you are not familiar with the periods of Israel's history, find an introduction to the Old Testament to help you understand them.

to worship and conduct their lives in relationship to and in covenant with God. Long before the church as we know it existed, the people of Israel were in relationship to God, though the way this took shape evolved over time. Walter Brueggemann has suggested that the Old Testament depicts three phases in Israel's self-understanding, and each phase relates to a particular context or situation in which it found itself.[6]

The first communal expression, the pre-monarchic model, or the time from Moses to King David (1250 BCE to 1000 BCE), Brueggemann equates to a "new church start." Much like a new church starting today, they were establishing their life in God, planting their community apart from the power structures and prevailing institutions of Egypt, and forming an alternative community. This community of God's people was also socio-economically marginalized. It did not have great resources and capacity but depended "on the movement of the Spirit to give energy, courage, and power."[7] Brueggemann also speaks of this pre-monarchic people as a "wilderness" community.

The second form of community is described by the monarchic model, and it is the Old Testament model of Israel that dominates our thinking. From 1000 BCE up to 587 BCE, the royal monarchy of David represented the height of Israel's glory. In this model, the church and state are united, which approximates a modern-day faith community or an established and culturally legitimized church. The monarchic model has a temple, a professional priesthood, kings who take the covenant with God seriously, and prophets who speak to the powerful when correction is needed. Brueggemann goes further in suggesting that this is the prevailing model of church in the West, and for Israel, the dissolution of this period came as a result of the people's failure to be obedient to God or live in a manner acceptable to God. Perhaps there is some parallel to be found in the decline of the contemporary church.

But there is yet a third model that Brueggemann sees in the Old Testament: the post-exilic model. This expression begins with the Babylonian exile in 587 BCE and continues through the return to Palestine and the creation of the second temple. At this point, the people of Israel did not have influence over the government; they tended toward cultural syncretism that eroded their unique identity; and they developed strategies for survival, including the recovery of memory, the practice of hope, and the centrality of the sacred texts. Brueggemann argues that the sacred texts served to preserve the people's identity and to allow for imaginative practices that could enable them to remain distinct from the Persians and Greeks.

 Describe the focal point of each of the three images as you read through their descriptions.

What do these Old Testament models of the community of faith suggest to us today? First, as we come to recognize the shifting nature of Israel's communal and covenantal identity, we see that faith communities evolve and respond to changing circumstances. The Scriptures testify to the historical and contextual nature of our life in God and the need to preserve that covenant even in the midst of sweeping changes. Second, these models press us to consider the ways in which the faith community was not a central force in the sociopolitical scheme of things for much of Israel's history. Even when those in power did not value or share Israel's identity as a people of God, the people of Israel found ways to survive, to practice hope, to keep alive the memory of this sacred history. This is not unlike our situation in Western Christianity today. Third, we should not miss the importance of the sacred texts as a source of identity and a source of ongoing interpretation and reinterpretation of our faithfulness to God and how that faithfulness is expressed in communal ways and through institutions. When we read the Scriptures, we begin to see that the community of faith has taken different shapes and forms in remaining faithful to God during times of historical change and transition.

The New Testament word for the church—though neither used by Jesus nor prominent in the gospels—is *ecclesia*, the gathered community that follows Christ. Originally, this Greek word was used to refer to a political assembly of Greek citizens, but it took on new meaning among the Christian faithful as those who were called out of the world and into this assembly in Christ. Despite this definition, the church has never been easily categorized and described. In fact, in the New Testament, the images and representations of the church are many and varied. In his classic work *Images of the Church in the New Testament*, Paul Minear identifies almost a hundred different images used to describe the church. Certainly, some of these are more prominent than others, but these images serve to create our understanding of the church and our identity as a people gathered in the name of Christ. But no matter how prominent a model may seem in our minds, the New Testament never fully develops any of the images of the church, and we might suggest that the church is a complex reality and that our language is inadequate to fully express its nature and purpose. At the same time, our understanding or modeling of the community of faith must have a quality of authenticity within the context of our particular genera-tion. There is no doubt that the way one model or image was characterized in the year 500 is not precisely the same as we might express it today. In this short overview, we will turn to just three of the prominent New Testament images of the church: the body of Christ, the community of salvation, and the community of the Spirit.

The image of the body of Christ is based upon 1 Cor. 12:12-31 and may be the most frequently invoked language for the church: "For just as the body is one and has many members, and all the members of the body, though many, are one body, so it is with Christ. For in the one Spirit we were all baptized into one body—Jews or Greeks, slaves or free—and we were all made to drink of one Spirit. Indeed, the body does not consist of one member but of many. Now you are the body of Christ and individually members of it" (12:12-14, 27). This is an organic, embodied, incarnational image of the church as a living, breathing organism. And more than that, this image portrays the church as the very presence of Christ in the world. The implications are clear: we are not to be hidden away in a building or inwardly focused, but actively going out into the world to represent Christ. Of course, the body of Christ is not just one's own congregation, but is the whole of the people of God, the communion of saints, both those living and those who have passed the threshold of bodily death. So the body of Christ is an image that represents the incarnation, the Word become flesh, the embodied presence of the living Christ in the world.

A second important New Testament image for the church is the community of salvation. Think of this as a living representation in continuity with the crucifixion of Christ. We claim that Christ died for our salvation, and the church continues to represent or re-present this salvific action. The church is where the sacraments are administered. Baptism, which incorporates us into the church, is among other things the washing away of sin and rising into new life, with the promise of eternal life, not death. Holy Communion, also called the Eucharist or the Lord's Supper, is a repeatable act of worship in which we, again, represent the salvation in Christ to all who are gathered. Traditionally, Christians have claimed that there is no salvation outside the church, as first stated by Cyprian in the third century. To be incorporated into the church by faith and baptism is to receive the offer and promise of salvation, though we also believe that in the church are both wheat and chaff, sheep and goats, the good fish and the bad in the same net. Thus, salvation is present within the church, but being present in the church is not a guarantee of salvation.

In contemporary theology, the church as the locus of salvation has undergone scrutiny, especially in relation to a pluralistic society. In other words, is salvation found only in Christ? If you answer "yes" to this question, you would hold an exclusivist position of salvation given only to believers in Christ. Yet if we begin to reflect upon the meaning of being "in Christ," this claim might not be as straightforward as we would initially think. Consider the fact that Dietrich Bonhoeffer, a traditional theologian in many ways, had a deep desire to visit India to meet Gandhi and to find

 Identify the four answers to this question of whether salvation is only in Christ.

where "Christ" is present in the East. Maybe Bonhoeffer held a position of inclusivism, which would suggest that the Christian revelation is definitive but followers of other religions may still receive salvation. We cannot be certain what Bonhoeffer intended by his hope to discover Christ in the East, but it seems clear that he did not expect to find the same understanding of Christ as dominates Western ecclesiology. If you answer that there are many paths leading to the same destination which is God, you would adhere to a position of pluralism. Of course, you could also argue for a position that suggests there are multiple, parallel paths leading to different destinations—all of which might be valid trajectories to wholeness.

So where do you stand on the question of salvation, and why do you find that particular position most persuasive? Does the church play a significant role in your understanding of where salvation is found? The church can be understood as the community of salvation, as the place—or a place—where redemption in Christ is offered again and again. The church, in this sense, takes on the form of the crucifixion, as the location of our salvation. Remember, that salvation points toward wholeness, toward the fullness of life seeping into our pores and enlivening our cells and molecules. So the church as the community of salvation indicates entering into the suffering of the world and engendering life in the face of death.

A third prominent New Testament image of the church is the community of the Spirit, which we can connect to the resurrection or the resurrected life. Returning to the text of Acts 2 and the story of Pentecost, the central or initiating action is the giving of the Spirit to the whole community, forming the community into one body. Saint Augustine referred to the Holy Spirit as the bond of love, not only within the Trinity, but also among believers within the Christian community. Without the Holy Spirit, the church remains a collection of separate individuals, but in the Spirit, we become rightly and radically related. So in this third image, the church is the community of the Spirit, a resurrected people given new life in the Spirit.

Now, these three images of the church have a christological shape—incarnation, crucifixion, resurrection—which suggests that the head, heart, life, energy, existence of the church is in and through Christ and his acts on our behalf and in the presence of the Holy Spirit. The church is God's community, more so than it is our own community, at least as a spiritual reality, which brings us to recognize that there are always tensions related to being the church, a point we alluded to earlier. Let's look briefly at two primary tensions that always exist for us as Christians: (1) spiritual and sociological and (2) communal and personal.

As noted at the outset of this section, the church always lives in the tension of being on the one hand a creation of God's, empowered by the Holy Spirit, formed by the acts of Jesus Christ and, on the other hand, simultaneously a broken, misguided human institution. Sometimes this is referred to in terms of the invisible and visible church. It is the difference between being a spiritual reality (that is, an expression of the very life of God in the world—in all the mystery of the divine) and a sociological reality, a human construction. Of course, we are always simultaneously both of these, and the church as a gathered people needs both the spiritual and the institutional dimensions to exist. We are the resurrected people, incorporated into Christ's body and offered the gift of salvation. Yet we are also people who have one foot in the old creation, sometimes bickering with one another, sometimes seeking to maintain the bureaucracy we have created as if it were God's own bureaucracy. The church lives in the tension of the spiritual and sociological, and the goal is to find a balance between the two realities.

Christian faith always has a second tension, which is the tension between the communal nature of our faith and the personal journey of discipleship. When we believe in Christ, we are inescapably incorporated into the church as a spiritual reality. The reality of God in Christ in the Holy Spirit is radically relational. *Radical* means "to the roots" or as it was in the beginning and is promised to be in the new creation. But at the same time, the journey of faith must be taken individually. I cannot believe for you, or you for me. Each of us must make that decision alone with God. And each of us must constantly throw down our nets—security nets, nets that entangle us, whatever they may be—so that we might continue to participate in the life of faith and in the church. We have no choice but to live in this tension between the communal and the personal and find a balance between the two.

A few other dimensions of the church and ecclesiology are important theological concerns. Most notable are the four "marks" of the church: one,

 Try to define each of the four marks with one or two words.

holy, catholic, and apostolic. When we proclaim that there is "one" church, we are pointing toward the unity of all believers, despite our denominational differences and even the schism between Catholic and Protestant or between Eastern and Western Christianity. We are all one in Christ. Of course, the boundaries for who is considered "in" and who is thought to be "out" depend upon where you stand in the Christian tradition. Although the unity seems tenuous in human terms, the church as God's community of faithful is nonetheless characterized by a real, albeit elusive oneness.

We, secondly, refer to the church as "holy." I have sometimes been struck by the entry on *holy* in *A New Handbook of Christian Theology*, edited by Musser and Price. When I turn to the definition of *holy*, the entry simply states, "See God." Indeed, there is something profound, if unintentional, in this directive to "see God" if we want to understand the meaning of holiness. Sometimes holiness is regarded as a condition of moral righteousness and integrity, and while it is that, holiness must be considered as a far richer term, if we are directed to God as the source and definition of the concept. To speak of holiness is to point toward the fullness of love, in keeping with the scriptural notion that God is love (1 John 4:8). The holiness of the church, then, consists in being set apart by God and to the service of God (a concept rooted in the Old Testament). It also suggests being in right relationship with God and thus able to embody in greater measure and share widely God's own love.

The third mark of the church is its catholicity or universality. The problem with this word, of course, is that many people understand "catholic" to mean the Roman Catholic Church, which leads them to revise the Apostles' Creed to read, "the holy universal church," rather than "the holy catholic church." The universality of the church indicates that it encompasses all times, all peoples, and all places. There are no geographical or physical boundaries to the church, no limits to where it exists and who may participate. There is one church numerically, but in its universality, it is unbounded and reaches across time and space. At times, of course, the institutional church has created boundaries and excluded people based upon race, language, and other physical characteristics. Even so, the catholicity of the church remains undiminished in the sight of God.

Finally, we point to the apostolic nature of the church. Apostolicity is a disputed concept, since for Roman Catholic and Eastern Orthodox Churches, it refers to a traceable relationship to the original followers (apostles) of Jesus, but for Protestants, it tends to mean a relationship to the apostolic witnesses and teachings found in the New Testament. For the Roman Catholic and Eastern Orthodox Churches, apostolic succession provides their priests and churches with a direct line of authority stretching back to the laying on of hands by the original apostles. From this basis of authority, these churches claim to be the true church. In the Protestant context, however, apostolicity is viewed more broadly in terms of those who follow the teachings of the apostles passed on through the scriptural witnesses and inspired by the Holy Spirit as the true mark of the church. Despite the differences in understanding apostolicity, the point is the same: that the church finds its origin and continuance in the witnesses to Jesus Christ and the handing down of those teachings.

It might be helpful at this point for you to reflect upon your understanding of the church, the images you use and the characteristics that form its fundamental identity. If members of the Millennial generation, people under thirty, tend to hold a dim view of institutions, how might you offer such a person an image or vision of the church as much more than a human institution, but without denying its flawed and broken character? In today's society, a clear and persuasive ecclesiology might prove to be a key element in the church's renewal and meaningfulness in a postmodern society.

I Believe in the Last Things

The doctrine of the "last things," eschatology, is perhaps the most difficult doctrine to articulate. A great deal can be said about eschatology, but at the same time, very little can be known with any confidence. In the cross and resurrection of Jesus, we find evidence of the promised deliverance from this life of suffering and death. This hoped-for end gives us courage and orients us across the span of our lifetime. Yet at the same time, so much of what we consider in this doctrine is highly speculative. What do we really know about the future? What does heaven look like, and will we have physical bodies? If so, what age will we be? When will the final judgment take place? Even questions about things such as whether our beloved pets will be in heaven cross our minds. We cannot answer these questions with any certainty. We can only know what God has revealed and promised to us through Christ and the scriptural witnesses. Nonetheless, if we were to strip away the hope that is found in Christian eschatology, our faith would be rudderless in this world.

Several topics fall within the doctrine of eschatology: the *parousia* (the second coming), the kingdom of God, the resurrection of the body, the final judgment, the life everlasting, heaven and hell, and others. But the central or perhaps unifying concept is Christian hope. We intentionally speak of

Christian hope to suggest that our hope is rooted and grounded in the living God as the unique source of our confidence and faith in a good future, despite the current realities in which we live. Hope, according to Heb. 6:19, is "a sure and steadfast anchor of the soul." Christian hope is anchored to

 Think about this metaphor of an anchor and how hope serves a similar function.

and grounded in the nature and promises of God, which not only point us toward a promised good future, but enable us to live with confidence in the present. Glenn Tinder expresses this idea succinctly: "The way we hope is the way we live."[8] More than one theologian has proposed that the doctrine of eschatology is centered in this anchoring function of hope.

While God should be considered the source of our hope, we can speak more specifically of eschatological claims that serve to buoy our hopefulness. First, the quality of our hope is supported by the promised second coming of Christ, the *parousia*, at which time God will complete the new creation, such that death and suffering will be no more (Rev. 21:4), the wolf will lie down with the lamb (Isa. 11:6), the child will play on the adder's den and not be harmed (Isa. 11:8), and every tear will be wiped away from every eye (Rev. 21:4). The *parousia* points beyond individual restoration toward God's cosmic plan for the reconciliation of the entire created order, a claim that is echoed in the belief in the resurrection of the body. The resurrection of the body reaffirms the goodness of creation and the wholeness or integrity of the human being as body, spirit, and mind. Thus, our hope in the resurrection of the body finds expression in this life as we experience some measure of healing and wholeness, which serves as a foretaste of the promised resurrection of the body to new life.

Of course, the resurrection of the body also connects to the concepts of life everlasting and heaven and hell, concepts that have been widely depicted over the centuries but with little evidence, other than a few scriptural references, upon which to base them. We hope in the new heaven and the new earth in which all things will be in right relationship with one another and with God. We understand heaven as a place of joy, well-being, peace, and love. Yet, too, Christians have traditionally held a belief in hell as the antithesis of right relationship and merited as a result of refusing God's grace and choosing to "go it alone" or to deny the need for God and others. In this sense, Migliore aptly defines hell as "self-destructive resistance to the eternal love of God."[9] Of course, we do not have a diagram or photograph that shows us the landscape of heaven or hell, though these concepts do symbolize that fundamental choice either to live fully in right relationship to God and others or to choose our own small and selfish desires as the fullest expression of life. Perhaps hell is a fiery inferno filled with weeping and gnashing of teeth. Perhaps heaven is a place with harps and white robes and angelic choruses singing alleluias. We simply do not know. So we are left with the free will to choose God or not, whatever the consequences may be. We are free to choose hope in God, which is bolstered by our belief in the *parousia*, the resurrection of the body, and the life everlasting. Why we need hope and God's promises leads us to the final doctrine we will discuss in this brief overview: theological anthropology.

The Doctrine of Humanity

You may have noticed that this last doctrinal section begins with a heading that differs from the others. It signals that the doctrine of humanity, or theological anthropology, is not a subject of our faith in the way the other doctrines are. We do believe in the fallenness of humanity, which was created in the image of God; we believe in our sinfulness as well, but we do not believe in ourselves as human beings. We are not the subject of our faith. In some respects, we are the problem for which the Christian faith is the answer. Even so, we are also fundamentally part of the answer, for we possess free will and the calling to represent the good news of Jesus Christ to others. I have saved the doctrine of theological anthropology for last simply because it turns our attention back upon ourselves, upon who we are and why we need God. This ordering of doctrines is, of course, a methodological choice, as described in chapter 3.

Christians believe that human beings are created in the image of God (in Latin, the *imago Dei*). We were created good, complete, and whole, as described in the creation stories. Genesis 1:27 is a defining text, claiming that we were created in the image and likeness of God. Theologians through the ages have understood this notion of the image of God in various ways, but generally it points toward a certain moral character and dignity in human beings that reflect the divine nature, if only in part. Sometimes, as well, the image of God is suggestive of the human capacity for reason and reflection, which is not present in the minds of other living creatures—at least, not to the extent that we possess. Though the image was lost or diminished in the fall from grace, Christians believe in the restoration of this image as part of the redemptive work of Jesus Christ and the empowerment of the Holy Spirit. Creation in the image of God tells us something about what it means to become fully human as God created us to be.

Yet the pervasive reality of sin undermines our created goodness and that image of God implanted in the human being. Sometimes I have heard Christians claim that they do not sin, by which they mean they do not engage in a list of prohibited behaviors such as smoking and drinking alco-

 Try to identify the various dimensions of sin articulated throughout this section.

holic beverages. This is, of course, a very narrow and incomplete rendering of the concept of sin. Among the Greek words that can be translated as sin, *hamartia* is the most common, and it derives from the notion of "missing the mark," as an arrow missing a target. In other words, to sin is to fall short, to miss the mark, to turn left when we should turn right. Sin is fundamentally about turning away from God and God's will or way for our lives. It is the rejection of the gift of grace. Sin can arise from either self-centeredness or self-denigration, thinking either too highly of ourselves or too little, and it can take the form of sins of commission (action) or omission (inaction).

As noted earlier in this book, the tradition has typically followed the teaching of Augustine that we human beings are not free not to sin, that there is a bondage of our will. How, then, does free will exist or function if our will is in bondage to sin? Tertullian was the first theologian to refer to free will or the human capacity to decide how we will conduct our lives. Augustine then developed the doctrine, explaining that we do have a measure of free will, even if it is limited by sin, and the restoration of our free will is possible only through God's grace. Sin is a universal condition, as Paul writes to the Romans: "all, both Jews and Greeks, are under the power of sin" (3:9). We are aided by God's grace in order to choose not to sin.

When we speak of the bondage of the will, we are also pointing toward the concept of original sin. Christians have long held that original sin is inherited as a result of the disobedience of the first people in the Garden of Eden. While some theologians dispute this belief in original sin, we might reframe it in contemporary terms as a genetic mutation that continues to be passed down to each successive generation. We are not as we were in the beginning. When we consider this inherited predisposition to sin, our attention is focused on the individual. Indeed, throughout most of Christian history, we have viewed sin as primarily an individual concept or something that needs to be addressed individually. The logic is well known: in our confession of Jesus Christ, our individual sins are forgiven.

Since the rise of liberation theologies in the 1970s and beyond, theologians and the church have begun to articulate a concept of systemic sin, in addition to individual sin. Systemic sin begins with the notion that the rejection of grace can be structured socially and not just individually. When we begin to reflect upon the systems and institutional arrangements that exist in our world, it becomes clear that sin is not reducible to individual choice alone. For example, suppose you stop at a coffee house and buy a double latte that costs you three or four dollars. If the seller does not indicate that this is fair-trade coffee, it might be the case that the farmers who grew the coffee beans earned pennies a pound for their product. You may feel you have done nothing wrong; all you did was purchase an expensive cup of coffee. But in doing so, you support a system that impoverishes the farmer in that distant country. If God seeks the flourishing and fullness of life for all people, then the system that diminishes the farmer's life is sinful, as is our participation in that system. Sinful systems are death-dealing rather than life-giving, which is the way of Jesus Christ. Examples of systemic sin abound, of course. But the point is an important one: sin has a structural dimension as it is woven into institutions of human making, including the church. No doubt, systemic sin is complex, since it is difficult to identify the sources of the sin, which are often interwoven in a network of actions and structures, and even more difficult to eradicate. It is also quite difficult for individuals to be conscious of the many ways in which we support sinful systems. Nonetheless, we are called by God to turn away from sin, which means helping to name systemic sin and reject its diminishment of some lives in order to further others. Perhaps you can think of additional examples of systemic sin that your church or you, yourself, have sought to change.

In our struggle to overcome personal and structural sin, Christians believe that God's grace, Christ's atoning work, and the empowerment of the Holy Spirit provide us with a certain freedom from the power and presence, the bondage, of sin. At the center or heart of this freedom is the freedom to be in right relationship with God, other human beings, and the whole of creation. In Christ, we are a new humanity renewed in the image of God, the goodness of our creatureliness, and the fullness of life lived in harmony and balance with all of God's creation. It is here in the midst of this vision of restored humanity and radical relationship that we come to embody and to share the ultimate gift of God's love that never gives up on us, even when we give up on ourselves or others. God is love, a love that never ends, a love qualitatively richer than any expression of human love, which is the final word in our journey through the doctrines of the Christian faith. When we reach the end of our thinking, acting, and being, this one thing remains: love.

 ## Questions for Personal Exploration

1. Reread the Apostles' Creed. Which of the beliefs do you struggle with, and why? Has your thinking changed about any of them in the reading of this chapter?
2. How do you understand the fullness of God? And how would you explain the Christian doctrine of one God who is known in three different ways?
3. Which of the doctrines discussed in the chapter do you find most difficult? And which do you find most comforting or illuminating?
4. What does it mean to be human from a Christian perspective?

 ## Resources for Deeper Exploration

There are a number of systematic theologies, any of which would add to your study of these doctrines. Listed here are just a few to consider.

Chopp, Rebecca S., and Mark Lewis Taylor, eds. *Reconstructing Christian Theology.* Minneapolis: Fortress Press, 1994.

Hodgson, Peter C., and Robert H. King, eds. *Christian Theology: An Introduction to Its Traditions and Tasks.* Rev. ed. Minneapolis: Fortress Press, 1994.

Jones, Serene, and Paul Lakeland, eds. *Constructive Theology: A Contemporary Approach to the Classical Themes.* Minneapolis: Fortress Press, 2005.

McGrath, Alister E. *Christian Theology: An Introduction.* 5th ed. Malden, MA: Wiley-Blackwell, 2010.

Migliore, Daniel L. *Faith Seeking Understanding: An Introduction to Christian Theology.* 3rd ed. Grand Rapids: Eerdmans, 2014.

👓 Notes

1. Langdon Gilkey, *Maker of Heaven and Earth: The Christian Doctrine of Creation in the Light of Modern Knowledge* (Garden City, NY: Anchor, 1965), 209–10.

2. Process theology, derived from the philosophy of Alfred North Whitehead by theologians such as Charles Hartshorne, John Cobb, and Marjorie Suchocki, suggests that God is, in fact, influenced by temporal processes and uses persuasion rather than coercion to further the divine mission in the world.

3. Elizabeth A. Johnson, *She Who Is: The Mystery of God in Feminist Theological Discourse* (New York: Crossroad, 1995), 131.

4. Ibid.

5. Ibid., 135.

6. Walter Brueggemann, "Rethinking Church Models through Scripture," *Theology Today* 48, no. 2 (July 1991): 128–38.

7. Ibid., 132.

8. Glenn Tinder, *The Fabric of Hope* (Atlanta: Scholars, 1999), 28.

9. Daniel L. Migliore, *Faith Seeking Understanding*, 2nd ed. (Grand Rapids: Eerdmans, 2004), 347.

Conclusion: Going Deeper

If you have reached this conclusion, then you have just completed your first journey along the flowing stream of theology. I hope you dove into that stream and let yourself be carried along to places you have not been before. I also hope you feel closer to God in some way because you have taken this journey. Did you see and encounter new things along the way? Were you startled by something strange or beautiful? Admittedly, theology is not the easiest discipline to learn, and in this short volume, we have only skimmed the surface. There is yet much for you to discover about this theological discipline and, especially, the teachings of our faith. In these last few pages, I want to introduce you to the idea of writing your own credo and offer you a few suggestions for the successful study of theology as you enter into your seminary program.

Credo

As we have seen, the Latin word *credo* means "I believe." It is not uncommon in schools of theology for students to write a credo or a comprehensive and systematic statement of what they believe. Sometimes it is a requirement of the systematic theology course; sometimes it is the capstone project for graduation. Even without the writing of a credo, the ability to articulate your beliefs will be central to your theological education.

While it might seem daunting, this short volume has equipped you with the tools necessary to embark upon the writing of a credo. I want to encourage you to take some time to write your first credo. Not only will it provide a point of comparison as your understanding grows in the years ahead, but it will also raise questions that you can carry with you into your seminary studies. Your first credo can take the form of one page on each doctrine, preceded by some methodological considerations, such as your sources. It can simply take the form of a detailed outline, as if you were preparing to write a paper. However you proceed, this exercise will reinforce the topics and vocabulary introduced to you in this book. I encourage you to take some time to reflect upon what you believe, then stash it away until you are halfway through seminary. You will be pleasantly surprised to discover how much you have grown in your understanding.

Suggestions for Further Study

As we approach the end of this short volume, I want to offer a few suggestions that may help you in the months and years to come, as you enter into seminary and the study of systematic theology. There are five keys that will assist you in unlocking the treasures of theology: openness, attentiveness, prayerfulness, questioning, and organizing.

Openness to hearing new ideas and exploring theological positions with which you might not agree is the first key. To be open to various theologies and doctrinal considerations without becoming defensive is a sign of a mature faith. Rather than needing to be defensive, we recognize that God can stand up to our scrutiny and, more importantly, that we will not lose our faith simply because we have examined it well. I encourage you to cultivate an openness to learn.

The second key for successfully navigating the study of theology is related to maintaining a posture of attentiveness. When I speak of attentiveness, I am suggesting that we need to listen carefully to the positions of authors, professors, and classmates as they articulate theologies that are unfamiliar or different from where we stand. When I teach students the theology of James Cone, I have them read one of his early essays that contains strong language and emotion. I warn them that they will encounter those things, but also encourage them to listen attentively for his argument and to consider the context in which he wrote that theological statement. Some students react so strongly to the language that they are not able to listen to his theological statement. For those who seek to be pastors, learning to listen carefully to others, even if we disagree, is an important skill.

One of the best ways I know to cultivate openness and attentiveness is to approach the practice of theology with an attitude of prayerfulness. When we learn to read theology as a spiritual practice, which brings us into deeper relationship with God and others, our study of theology becomes a form of prayer. Whenever you begin to read a theology book or essay, consider it the work to which God has called you. You may be called to ministry, but first you are called to a time of preparation. Thus, instead of viewing your theological education as a rite of passage or a hurdle you must cross, see each class and reading as a process of formation for the sacred task of ministry. Through an attitude of prayer, we remind ourselves that God is present, and we ask the Holy Spirit to illuminate our minds as we read and learn.

The fourth key to the study of theology has been introduced to you throughout this book: questioning. Theology is a questioning discipline. As we noted, the more we study, the more questions we are likely to have. Whenever you read theology or listen to a theology lecture, you should begin by asking as many questions as you can about the subject. Sometimes seminarians, pastors, and Christians in general believe that faith in God requires definite and concrete answers. But as we have seen, Jesus may have been the questioner-in-chief. If we follow his model, asking questions will become a habit or spiritual discipline that will guide us into deeper, more thoughtful answers about the life of faith.

Lastly, the successful study of theology depends upon a certain capacity to organize. Not only do we organize our thoughts so the doctrines we share make sense and are meaningful, but we also organize the various pieces of theology into a coherent whole. The ability to discern how one doctrine relates to the next, which biblical texts provide warrants for one teaching or another, and within which stream of the tradition someone stands requires this capacity for organizing. If you have not yet developed skills for organizing your life and studies, now would be a good time to do so. Bringing some order out of chaos will take you a long way in the study of God and the Christian faith.

Our journey together ends here, but I hope these five keys and the map provided in this book will assist you in navigating the road that lies ahead. Much like the disciples traveling to Emmaus in Luke 24, you may not realize it at first, but the resurrected Christ is waiting to accompany you, to engage you in conversation, and to open your eyes to see the very presence of God.